MERIDIAN

*Crossing Aesthetics*

Werner Hamacher

Editor

Translated by
Charlotte Mandell

*Stanford
University
Press*

———

*Stanford
California
2003*

# FRAGMENTS OF THE ARTWORK

*Jean Genet*

Assistance for the translation was provided by
the French Ministry of Culture.

The material on pages 171–72 is an
extension of this copyright page.

Cette ouvrage, publié dans le cadre d'un programme
d'aide à la publication, bénéficie du soutien du
Ministère des Affaires étrangères et du Service
Culturel de l'Ambassade de France.

This work, published as part of a program of aid for
publication, received support from the French Ministry
of Foreign Affairs and the Cultural Services of the
French Embassy in the United States.

Stanford University Press
Stanford, California

Printed in the United States of America
on acid-free, archival-quality paper.

Library of Congress Cataloging-in-Publication Data

Genet, Jean, 1910–1986
    [Fragments ... et autres textes. English]
    Fragments of the artwork / Jean Genet.
        p.   cm. — (Meridian, Crossing Aesthetics)
    ISBN 0-8047-4286-3 (alk. paper)—
    ISBN 0-8047-4287-1 (alk. paper : pbk.)
    I. Title. II. Series.
PQ2613.E53F7313    2003
844'.912—dc21                                    2002014202

Original Printing 2003

Last figure below indicates year of this printing:
12   11   10   09   08   07   06   05   04   03

Designed by Susan Riley
Typeset by Tim Roberts in 10.9/13 Adobe Garamond

# Contents

# Translator's Acknowledgments

Translators live on the kindness of the Other (not least of all the authors themselves, to whom we owe our profession), and I would like to name a few of the others here: Odile Chilton, Mark Cohen, Helene Tieger and Jane Hryshko of the Bard Library, William Mullen, Jennifer Cazenave, Olivier Brossard, Yan Brailowsky of the French Embassy in New York, Helen Tartar and the editorial staff at Stanford University Press, and of course, my husband, Robert Kelly, who spent many hours reading and rereading the manuscript and making valuable comments and suggestions.

# FRAGMENTS OF
# THE ARTWORK

'adame Miroir

*to Ginette Sénémaud*

*Description of a ballet*
*danced by Messrs*
ROLAND PETIT, SERGE PERRAULT,
*and* SKOURATOFF
*to a musical score by*
DARIUS MILHAUD

SCENE: The set represents the interior of an extremely sumptuous palace; the hallways are covered with beveled mirrors. The place where the ballet is to be danced is a sort of crossroads where these very bright avenues meet. On the ceiling, rich, heavy chandeliers. No fabric on the walls, just gold, marble, glass.

THE TITLE: I want only to indicate this amusing fact: when I had just completed the play, I found the title "Madame Miroir," but the idea of such a ridiculous carnival prevented me from using it seriously. As a joke, I pronounced it for myself with a working-class accent, dragging out the "a's" and the final "oir," and, as in Belleville, I elided the initial "M." It seemed silly to write it that way, but I obtained a distortion of the word "madame" that gave "adam" in which a feminine past and possibility could also be read: "adam" was, in a rather foggy mirror, the blurred, deformed image of an object having certain qualities.

THE MAIN CHARACTER: He is a sailor who has no past. His life begins with the choreography, which utterly contains it. He is young and handsome. He has curly hair. His muscles are hard and supple: in short, he is our idea of the ideal lover. He is dressed in

I

the summer outfit of the sailors of the National Marine: white.
Polished black shoes, with very supple soles. A rose is slipped by
its stem into his leather belt.

THE DOMINO: It would be too easy to see Death in it. It is not
death. Who, then? The author does not know. It is a domino of
purple silk, gloved in black, whose essential accessory is a black
crêpe fan.

THE CHOREOGRAPHY: The domino enters from a hallway on the
right. One hand shading his eyes (the other holds the crêpe fan),
he inspects the room, then turns his back and crosses the stage,
examining each mirror *in which his Image does not appear*, going
all the way back, to the left, where a hallway begins and he will
disappear.

This character's movements must be slow and very supple. He
gives the impression of being carried by a moving walkway. His
gestures with the fan toward the mirrors are very familiar. He
seems, sometimes, to be dusting a plinth with it, or a caryatid.

The domino having exited, light floods the scene, which
remains empty for a few seconds.

The music plays a very light waltz, a sort of *java* [a popular
dance—*Trans.*].

Where the domino exited there appears, cigarette butt in his
lips, a sailor.

During the entire dance, the sailor's face will remain impassive
(*he would be handsomer if he danced first with his eyes closed*) but
when he appears (*going backward*), his gestures indicate fear. He
retreats with tiny steps; and bumps against a mirror. He turns and
sees his image. He runs to another mirror, where he again sees his
image. (*A dancer, placed behind a mirror-shaped frame—veiled
with organdy—has the role of the reflection, copying the sailor's poses
in reverse.*)

With one mirror after the other, desperate, the sailor will collide, always bumping into his Image. Terrified, he dances alone, to an increasingly fast rhythm, until, exhausted, losing his cap, he falls to the ground, where he continues a sort of miserable crawling. Then he raises himself a bit and looks at one of the mirrors.

In this mirror (*the one at right, near the set*) the gestures of the Image do not seem to correspond exactly with the sailor's. The sailor gets worried. He creeps up to it, visibly mistrustful. While he is still crouching, the Image is already standing, at the edge of the mirror. The sailor stands up completely, and, with a sort of tender resignation, goes toward it. The Image then copies his last gestures. The sailor passes a hand over the mirror, as if to wipe away the condensation he has just made with his mouth. The Image performs the same gesture. Finally the sailor punches in the direction of the mirror, but instead of meeting glass, the hand strikes the chin of the Image, whose head sways. The sailor brings both hands forward, the Image does the same, the sailor steps back, the Image steps back; the sailor again approaches, the Image approaches; the sailor steps back, but this time the Image advances and emerges from the mirror.

A dance begins (*first a pursuit*), the sailor and his Image, during which the mirrors stop reflecting.

THE PURSUIT: The Image, while dancing, tries to approach the sailor, who runs away, terrified. But at a certain point, the sailor, out of breath, is forced into an angle of the mirror (*fully visible to the audience*). Courageously, and a little intrigued, he faces his Image and walks toward it. In its turn, the Image flees. Finally, little by little, while turning their backs to each other, they touch, turn, and embrace. Kiss each other on the mouth. The Image takes the sailor's cigarette butt in his mouth.

THE DANCE: They dance. The same light waltz of the beginning, which they perform with little steps, like the sailors in dance
halls: a very stylized waltz.

The two dancers try to evoke a lovers' chase. They take each
other by the neck, then let go, dance cheek to cheek. They seldom
let go of each other.

In the choreography she designed, Mlle. Janine Charrat made
the Image lift the sailor (*from behind*) and let him down, then
continue to dance. I will keep this idea, with this addition: lying
on the floor, the sailor rolls over, crossing the whole stage from
right to left. Standing in front of him, watching him (*and facing
the audience*), the Image moves with him, slowly, the four feet in
harmony in these vertical and horizontal movements.

The rest of the dance must be extremely lustful. Erotic. The two
dancers delicately perform the gestures familiar to sailors: raise their
trousers with the flat of their hands, hook their thumbs into their
leather belts, turning suddenly to present their profile, stretching,
emphasizing their thigh and arm muscles, hands in their pockets to
stretch the cloth on their fly, hang by their arms, etc.[1]

The dancers are on the point of uniting when, through the
doorway where he had disappeared, the domino enters.

DEATH: As soon as he enters (*his walk still supple and slow*), the
dancers become anxious. Nonchalantly, the domino advances. He
seems to ignore them. He lingers (*fan in front of his face*) at the
mirrors, but sure enough, he comes toward the defeated couple,
who are separating. Finally the domino separates the sailor and
his Image (*the domino's gestures as casual as possible*). The sailor
and his Image dance finally with the domino. A frenzied waltz,
more and more turbulent. The domino is carried in turn by the
sailor and the Image, sometimes by both.

Finally the domino makes a decision and chooses the sailor. He
pursues him for a bit, then stabs him with the closed fan. During

the execution, the Image is leaning on an upright and observes the scene without showing any emotion. Finally the domino takes the prostrate sailor by his hair and pulls him into the wings, where they disappear.

For a few seconds, the Image dances alone, with a step that indicates solitude and panic. More precisely, it dances while moving backward.

THE METAMORPHOSIS: The domino returns. He pursues the Image, which escapes. Finally he traps it and dances with it, an extremely violent dance. The domino seems more and more menacing. He tries to make the Image enter one of the mirrors in the back. The Image resists and flees. Around the center of the set, the domino meets up with it. Not to the spectators, but to the Image alone, the domino, removing the fan, shows his face. The two dancers examine each other. By the agitation of their legs, their attitudes, we feel that they are tackling each other, are confronting each other. Finally the Image gives way. The domino takes its hand and, facing the audience, slips his long black glove onto the Image's hand (*choose a glove of silk jersey*). One hand gloved, the Image escapes and dances alone, but scarcely has it taken a few steps when it returns, without the domino having moved, to the domino's side. The domino takes the sailor's other hand and slips the second glove onto it, then, with a double spinning movement, as the domino removes his robe, the Image clothes himself in it. (*The robe is just a long band of purple cloth.*) When the Image is dressed in the robe, it hides all but the head of the domino behind it. Finally, an arm (*clothed in white*) of what had been the domino offers, from behind the Image (*to the Image thus dressed in purple*), the fan. Then the character (*ex-domino*) reveals himself completely: it is the sailor from before. (*When the domino dragged him into the wings, a dresser quickly got him into the purple robe, so it is he who came on the stage to exchange costumes with the Image.*)

The domino pursues the sailor. The sailor runs away. He tries to go back into a mirror, without ever being reflected in it. The mirrors resist. Finally he is joined by the domino, with whom he dances. The sailor again escapes. The domino throws himself into the pursuit. The sailor tries again one last mirror (*the one from which the Image had come*) and, slowly, backward, he penetrates the mirror.

The domino wants to follow him into it. Separated by the frame of the mirror, both dancers give in to a slight struggle. Finally, as if to take a better jump, the domino steps back. With the same gestures the sailor steps back, disappearing from the audience's eyes (*as a reflection withdraws from its subject, if the subject is removed*). The domino makes a leap that throws him against the mirror, but instead of meeting the sailor there, with a similar leap, it is his own reflection (*a purple domino*) that he strikes against. Surprised, he steps back. His reflection steps back. The music stops. The domino, then, with the same gestures he had at the beginning of the performance (*one hand shading his eyes*) examines the room, then the scene, the set, the palace. He sees the sailor's cap, the only sign of what must have happened. He leans down and picks it up, then continues his path to the back of the stage, but now each of the mirrors reflects the Image of a similar Image.

Finally, the backdrop being a prop in the form of a double mirror, without anyone seeming to move it, this door opens as the domino approaches it, following his rhythm. His movement is as described above, and, after he crosses the doorsill, since the floor slopes down, his body disappears like a ship's mast over the horizon. The curtain falls.


A FEW DETAILS OF EXECUTION: The dancers must dance keeping close to the ground. They never leap. Their gestures are exaggeratedly heavy.

When the Image comes out of the mirror, it does not step over the frame, but a sloping surface must allow it to *descend* from the mirror without raising its feet.

The three dancers work for a long time to achieve a sort of similarity of gestures.

This entire melodrama must give the impression of a game. To that end, the dancers charge their gestures with outré intentions: obscene, villainous, criminal.

No irony. It is a ballet for the Grand-Guignol. The domino will be a band of cloth that is wrapped like a sari. He wears shoes with rather high heels. Even when he dances and kills the sailor, he must give the impression of being asleep.


THE MUSIC: A series of accordion waltzes or cleverly stylized popular *javas* in which the accordion and harmonica are dominant. Music that is called "nostalgic."


This ballet was danced by M. Roland Petit to choreography by Mlle. Charrat.

The idea came to me at the Montmartre fair, in front of a sort of Palace of Mirrors in which the onlookers seemed imprisoned, bumped into their own image, and seemed incapable of finding the exit. I remembered a similar scene of which I had been the troubled witness, in Anvers, long ago. Superimposing in my mind the two episodes moved me, and, in a few minutes, I worked out the ballet I have just described.

## § 2    Letter to Leonor Fini

A "pestilential" smell: this can be recognized, by a wide-open nostril, as being composed of a thousand scents, interwoven, yet distinct according to each level and layer, in which you might find ferns, mud, the corpses of pink flamingos, salamanders, marsh reeds, a population of heavy scents, at once salubrious and harmful.

If they had to arrange themselves and make themselves visible, these scents would choose the hesitant, though precisely distinct forms of your drawings and paintings (this open nostril, you have painted it, and on it, on its cartilages, you have lingered for a long time, neglecting every other part of the face, above all you have taken note of its quivering. You wanted it to breathe in your—breathable—work and the exquisite and poisonous smell of your work).

If I fasten on the olfactory sense to speak about them, it is not because your drawings *immediately* evoke a smell (the way a certain music evokes a way of walking, for instance), but their complexity and their architecture seem to me comparable to the complex architecture of swamp odors.

Your work hesitates between vegetable and animal—mosses, lichens, as well as the most ancient animal representations following the most ancient method: the Fable.

But, aside from the fact that it is in the humid undergrowth that we might discover your giant orchids and your dwarf sphinxes being born—and, with difficulty, freed—from a fog itself born from an antediluvian nostril—where they proliferate and breed a dazzling universe—this smell seems to contain a smell of carnal humus and elemental plants.

Your person, Mademoiselle, which seems thus not to be painted, but depicted (de-picted), is almost obscenely akin to these two elements, vegetable and animal. The very sex of your young heroes rests, calm, in a tranquil moss. You are the marriage of plant and animal.

If your flora are *copied*, however, your fauna are invented. In fact, your paintings represent actual flowers and imaginary animals. But what dominates above all—the major scent that I have recognized—is that of death. The choice of colors, the anxiety of scenes, the meeting of a shell with a mirror, the folds of cloth, your masks—everything, in your work, bears witness to an intimate, macabre theater. Your paintings are sprinkled with ash. Like lichen on the trunk of a fallen tree, a skeleton's long hair continues to grow. Everything smells of death, the high boredom of an afterlife or an incalculable age.

They talk, with justice, about your technique: your perfect drawing is the sign of a refined civilization nostalgic for a life, not underground, but elemental, the one we can guess at in the depths of the oldest forests, the decomposition of which produces will-o'-the-wisps, those nymphs scarcely liberated from tree bark. It is, no doubt, in order to dominate this luxuriant, burgeoning, invading universe that you compel yourself to an exact precision about the color and shape of your objects. That is the only thing that allows you to confine the flood of seaweed, sirens, reptiles, that, tugging you by the hem of your dress, try to drown you. The technique of your drawing is thus supremely prudent.

Madame, I also see in it some kind of subtle science, and a sort of cunning—to give us only a polished image, a reflection, of your private adventure. But these characters—sphinxes, griffons, chimeras—who were once the supporters of a coat of arms or a wall hanging, now stop being decorative. They have devoured the humans they used to serve, who had tamed them, and in their turn, they sprawl in the sheets, chew rare herbs.

The era you live in is the Renaissance: I mean that you illustrate a theme that, historically, is called the Italian Renaissance. The splendor of this era is the same as that of your work, voluptuous and sprinkled with arsenic. Your ladies stretched out in the boudoir, their elegant boys are imprisoned, are stricken with a plague that comes from the highest Antiquity.

But a study has an aim: to reduce the work of the artist to a simple expression, or, as the philosophers say conceptually, a lived experience; to give or extricate the meaning of the work, to reestablish its relationships with the world and its time.

If you so firmly hold the bridle of the fabulous and shapeless animal that is erupting in your work and perhaps in your person, it seems to me, Leonor, that you very much fear letting yourself be carried away by savagery. You go to the masked ball masked in a cat's muzzle, but dressed like a Roman cardinal—you keep to appearances, lest you get lost in the sphinx's rump, and sprout her wings and claws. Wise prudence: you seem to me on the edge of metamorphosis. But if you tolerate any advice at all, I will advise you to stay not so long in the human world, in order to return to those dreams in which you call your sisters, the ivy-imprisoned nymphs. Do not think, Leonor, that I am joking: Stop the game of appearances: appear.

This aquatic, feverish world, stagnating in a jar, I feel it rush up to the luminous surface where it will be annihilated, I mean up into the intelligence that faces have. I will explain, but I needed that confused sentence: the whole mystery of a vegetable-animal conspiracy seeks to be resolved in a purified countenance, in a face.

Everything that seems to lurk at your heroes' feet, everything that tries to adorn them and comes near them, brushes against them, soils them, all that stagnates or bursts in the dark, climbs slowly up and becomes purer and purer in order, finally, to explode softly in a look or a smile. So I foresee an era when your faces will be rich, secretly fed by all those dramas that must remain invisible, swallowed up, eaten by your heroes. One day, the hand-somest of your portraits, having devoured it, will dream your work, that theatrical part of your work: then you will be a great classical painter.

Explaining your future method to you, my impertinence suddenly becomes apparent to me. But I am a poet who knows that the work of art must resolve the drama, not display it. These rags, these holly trees that destroy them, these animals, these flowers, these sumptuous diseases, these personified passions—I want them to be legible only in the break or the curve of lines of the clearest face. Your science of drawing and color is too great, and too rich, and multiplies the drama that preoccupies you, for your portraits not to be profoundly aware of it. Of all your phantasmagorias, only an upheaval in profundity will remain in the features, resembling something like a trembling shadow over your work. I know that your great honesty will make you continue not by the easiest way, but by the most dangerous.

Forgive me, Madame, I am hastening toward conclusions that displease you perhaps, but I want you to be worthy of being presented in that tiny room in the Louvre where there hang two portraits by Dürer, two by Cranach, and two by Holbein. I wish you, Madame, immense difficulties.

I have noticed, too, the silence of your canvases, the silence they establish, the silence of the links they represent, finally, the silence of your heroes. A Japanese fish makes me think of it. Like one, you seem to move in an element so sensitive that any shock, if it were not covered with felt, would take on the proportions of thunder. Like your pieces of cloth, the transparent fins of the fish I am looking at—oh, but you evoke the entire subterranean world, seaweed and pebbles!—have the same appearance as the feigned sleep of a cat. They are on the lookout. We suspect them. That at least is what I feel when faced with them.

I wonder to what this silence corresponds when I compare it to the chattering loquacity of the Italian artist. In your person everything moves: the eye, the breast, the foot, and, excuse me, the tongue. But you paint a mute world. Silence, crime, incest, poison, death, venom, smells, church, cenotaph, reptile, sea, roots, anxiety—I jot down, haphazardly, the elements of a theater that is pursued—or prepared for?—even in your daily life, but then, in a merely verbal way. Where does the actual performance take place, then? I pose an indiscreet question.

As to these slaves, these shaved convicts, where do they come from? What penal colonies do you pull them from, or rather, where do you cast them? For I cannot believe that they serve only as decorations for your games. They are not pretext, but end. Too much pathos is expressed by gestures that are paradoxically clear and empty (where, among the slaves in one picture, you have placed the most angelic azure); by their mouths, open—if they are breathing out—or closed if they persist in their scorn; by their cropped skulls.

At the final boundary of your work, then, you are preoccupied with the condemned world where silence has the power of aesthetic necessity. Maybe that is what will let you rejoin the most earthly, most "human," most carnal unhappiness. If, till these final days, you have given a solemn life to the most elegant wax candles, perhaps you will confer unhappiness and life on the lowly peat fire.

On the surface of your world swim all sorts of chignons that—allow me this coarseness—seem to me as much vomited as painted. I do not know how to speak accurately of hair and the effect it has on us, except that we recognize that it sickens us at the same time as it charms us. But you use hair to both these ends, simultaneously. We want to caress these curls, but also to get rid of them with disgust. Cut—and curiously these days, in your most recent paintings—the most beautiful, purest, most luminous heads appear, not only in their brilliant baldness, but also—despite sadness—with brighter eyes and fresher smiles or pouts. I have the tactlessness to see in them the quest to strip bare the physical, the social, in favor of an inner richness.

No doubt, other bald people, sumptuously dressed, stroll about in your old dreams, but I want to see them like the signs of a scattered, but violent asceticism. Convicts, the downtrodden, hard-luck men wandered about in your world of cloth and flowers: you recognized them, separated from the rest, and now you pay special attention to them.

We are free to interpret as we like, to use, and make them serve us, these signs that we have just chosen: for me, these heads of hair were the signs of the earthly world; these shaved skulls were signs of the most terrible curse and signs of inner realms where those still adorned with physical accoutrements no longer have any right to look, so I choose for you this more difficult procedure: the song of the living dead.

The idea of convict and punishment was already contained— implicitly understood—in those scenes of draperies powdered with arsenic, in that world of poisoners and infanticides; today, it finally manifests with an ironic precision. It is this idea that we want to exploit. And surely, if it denies us the possibilities of a more human, more social attractiveness, it may still let us discover the riches of the curse.

But I was speaking of dream. Your work seems to belong to it, but not entirely. It has to do, rather, it seems to me, with vague and vaguely directed daydream, now toward the vegetal and now toward more refined forms of culture. It was easy enough for you to take these daydreams as a starting point and then embellish them, to invent forms and imagine scenes, but now, starting from these shaved heads, it seems to me that your awareness will become greater and your attention more thoughtful. It is not only to form that you should bring the particular logic of the artist; it is in you yourself that you must seek out this unhappiness that we recognize in your new heroes, since you uncrowned them.

It is perhaps only the despair that your heroes express that will allow you to invent a profusion of new forms, in order, precisely, to retransmit it to us, transformed—and, I dare assert—in the form of a celebration. That the disillusioned smile—and it alone—the sorrowful look, the pout, the scar, will be a pretext no longer for a sad, fixed drama, which is waiting for who knows what speech to go on, but for an actual gala, not only of shadows and forms, but also of joy: that is the miracle of poetry.

Of course, you will find that I quickly picked out what is closest to me, and that it is first my own fault that I exalt. But would I be so passionate about a work if I had not discovered in it, from its very formation, not what I am heading toward already—and that will belong only to me—but those same desperate elements scattered throughout funereal ceremonies?

In short, till now, what have you been doing? On canvases, sometimes the world of your daydreams, sometimes that of your dreams, you have offered us a representation of them. If such an occupation allowed you to perfect your artistic gifts, it is only as you bring yourself up to date about a desperate world that we will understand your poetry. There exists a moral realm. It is absolutely the only one where it matters that the artist discover it by means of form. But it is the most perilous and noblest moral domain that interests us—as to its nobility, no preexistent law instructs us, we must invent it. And it is our entire life that we must conform— make conform—to this invention. To say it quickly, it is toward sanctity that, through your art, we want to see you move.

These convicts' heads—or what evokes them in your work—are themselves charged with a darkness as thick as the one that floats in your paintings and confuses the numerous elements in them, but it is not the same. Here is where we can speak of the darkness of the heart, when earlier you had mostly exploited the world's night.

"One day the most handsome portraits will dream your work," I wrote earlier. I think it's done. Those shaved heads have become iridescent with the scenes they glimpse and that your hands have fixed in a solemn eternity. The troublemakers of your dramas, you have made them climb back up out of your penal colonies—where you had cast them—in order not to perish there, but to complete the drama. For it is they, isn't it, who are responsible for these sumptuous orgies? The expression "a cruel goodness" seems to me to be apt to designate this period of yours. By welcoming it and coming to terms with it, you do not relinquish your riches from before. These adhere all too much to you, they are all too much your prehistory, and your convicts—or executioners—your indestructible ambiguity already makes them float, tremble, vacillate. Truly, they are not guilty of mere earthly crimes, they carry in them responsibility for your most intimate dismemberment. Not one child in your world. We look in vain for an innocent gaze; all are charged with a knowledge that is undoubtedly only the science and anxiety of the artist, for whom original purity does not exist. It is earned. And already your slaves have the sadness not of the evil they are going to perform—or, like your previous characters, that nostalgia for an evil that they do not have the strength to attempt—but that light and profound melancholy of men who have nothing left to do but organize, like a celebration, a life that is placed beyond despair.

I was able to take even more joy speaking about these magnificent images, each of which could be the projection of what I would have liked to become.

What do you want? What are you looking for? Flowers, animals, you already knew how to show them *outside* their uses as flower and animal, that is to say, as innocence. They all bear the mark of a voluntary crime. Fortunately. Thanks to that—to that charm over us—you will no doubt avoid the penal colony to which you seemed to me to be destined.

## § 3   Jean Cocteau

Greek [*Grec*]! The dry elegance of this word, its brevity, its rupture even, a little abrupt, are the qualities that can be readily applied to Jean Cocteau. The word is already a fastidious work of cutting: thus it designates the poet freed, cut loose from a substance whose chips he has made vanish. The poet—or his work, but even so, it is still he—remains a curious fragment, brief, hard, blazing, comically incomplete—like the word "Greek"—and one that contains the virtues that I want to enumerate. Luminosity above all. An illumination, above all uniform and cruel, showing precisely the details of a landscape apparently without mystery: that is Hellenic Classicism. The intelligence of the poet, in fact, illumines his work with such a white, raw light that it seems cold. This work is elegantly disordered, but each of its shafts or plinths was rigorously worked over, only, it seems, to be broken and left there. Today, beautiful foreigners visit it. It bathes in a very pure, very blue atmosphere.

It is not just playfulness that makes us, in speaking of Jean Cocteau, develop a metaphor. The word "Greek" was chosen by him, and he often sought to illustrate or refer to Greece as a whole. That is because he knows the darkest, most subterranean, wildest, almost insane aspects of what it signifies. From *Opéra* to *Renaud et Armide*, we guess these columns and broken temples to be the visible form of a pain and despair that chose—not to express themselves—but to hide themselves, by fertilizing it, beneath a gracious appearance, one that is a little mundane, since it seems understood that the noble collapse of Hellas belongs to a frivolous world. That is the tragedy of the poet. A deep human humus, almost foul-smelling, exhales whiffs of heat that sometimes make us red with shame. A sentence, a verse, a drawing of a very pure, almost innocent line in the interstices between words, at the point of intersection, emit like smoke a heavy, almost fetid air, revealing an intense subterranean life.

That is how Jean Cocteau's work seems to us, like a light, aerial, stormy civilization hanging from the heavy heart of our own. The very person of the poet adds to it, thin, knotted, silvery as olive trees.

But to have borrowed such forms was dangerous, for the least-developed minds came up with the notion of pastiche; while others even worse, gravely pondered this elegance alone and not what summoned it. So today, here, we want to draw your attention not to the way in which the poet hides himself, but to what it is he seeks to hide. Poems, essays, novels, theater—the entire body of work cracks, and lets anguish be discovered in the fissures. A vastly complex and sorrowful heart wants both to hide and to blossom. Is it a profound intelligence that makes this work infinitely sad? It trembles. We know that our images aren't very precise, but when expressions like "heavy chagrin," "profound despair," "wounded heart" are uttered, what remains to be said? As soon as we see a man's pained face—sternly in command of his pain, managing to transform it harmoniously—how can one speak with precision without a wounding pedantry? Jean Cocteau? He is a very great poet, linked to other poets by the brotherhood of the brow, and to men by the heart. We again insist on that, for it seems that a deplorable misunderstanding has developed about it. The grace of his style had to become the prey of what the world thinks of as the basest thing: the elite.

Which wanted to monopolize, make its own, this elegant form, neglecting the delicate bitter almond it contains. This time, though, we violently refuse this compromise and come to claim our rights over a poet who is not light, but serious. We deny Jean Cocteau the stupid title of "enchanter": we declare him "enchant-ed." He does not charm: he is "charmed." He is not a witch, he is "bewitched." And these words do not serve just to counter the base frivolity of a certain world: I claim that they better express the true drama of the poet.

Others besides me, cleverer, more learned, will speak to you of Jean Cocteau's place in literature, of his influence on Letters and on several generations, of his style and of the transparency of his poetry; as for me, I am concerned only with his heart, cultivated according to a rigorous morality and producing that rare plant: goodness. You understand: I am speaking of the quality that is more intelligence than sensibility, that is extreme comprehension. It was no doubt pursued and attained at the same time as the per-fection of style that testifies to it. I call on you to try to find, word by word, line after line, the severe—parallel—progression of the purity of the writing and of moral honesty. Jean Cocteau never gives us shameless lessons on morality—if he had to advise us, per-haps it would be with a malicious smile, the opposite of morality, but his sentence is constructed with such a respect for verbal sub-stance that this attitude, which is presence of mind, remains every time. It is then the rarely faltering rigor of a way of life that I invite you to discern in this style. Lightness, grace, elegance are qualities that refuse laziness and weakness, but what would they be if they were not applied to the hardest materials? But unlike the workman who, out of preference, chooses marble, the poet, by the choice of his method and his words, creates marble. Earlier we spoke of Greece. You will understand now: it was a matter of this new mar-ble: the moral idea we shape from it.

# § 4   Fragments ...

*The pages that follow are not extracts of a poem: they ought to
lead to one. This is a still-distant approach to one, since it is only
one of several drafts of a text that will be the slow, measured
progress toward the poem, justification of this text as the text will
be of my life.*

— J.G.

## Fragments of a Discourse

The morose eyelid—where the chimera was broken, you were
keeping watch.[1] But, from my darkness miraculously won, for my
sheets, now you are coming to lick me from outside, still naïve,
still hesitant: the kid and the young cavalier, the girl and the sun,
the rose and the boy, the moon and death—at every instant
another metamorphosis—death and this book. To whom if not
you, to talk about you in order to establish—all the way to mutu-
al downfall, echoes always more muted—a useless dialogue?
About your person: here are the worst features. Take refuge in the
horror of this text first, then in our confusion, then in a solitary
region, beyond reach, in Legend, if you dare. Or, find the route
of my humors: blood, tears, sperm, for my most secret orgasm,
curl up in it and in this cyst begin again your one-eyed vigil. To
discover what? You are rotting. To come back? How, unless I swal-
low you?

Sign, unalterable face, whose absolute content is death! To be
surrounded by it, a perfection that, from within, the occasion
seeks. Each of your steps—your long, nervous strides—could bear
your name. A subtle ankylosis distinguishes each one from a walk

that carries you to the coffin. Shameless and handsome, spitting your gobs of spit into the street, by dint of the beauty and shame-lessness that well up from your youth and your cough, be the provocation that walks and vanishes. Your step! Death marks it. And it plumbs your eyes. Apart from yours, what vices can be magnificently illustrated, brought to incandescence? Shame— whore, thief, consumptive—by force of shame comes respect. For you and for your sole use, write your legend. Clever at polishing yourself, your heart no longer beating, in no matter what posture death defines you. Monumental, complete in all movements, you are surrounded by death. Sliced apart, each of your steps can be put on display in a shop window. You, still among us, traveling our streets, may you be named, insolent and victorious strumpet, who are going, by the power of your nerve alone and your beauty, to take refuge mechanically in the sky of History.

When the idea is extinguished, the word sparkles with all its abandoned possibilities. It is empty. The idea is finished. Today— in this place—useless for any future act, the idea is fixed, sterile. Wives and daughters of kings, Phaedra, Antigone, dead, then leg-endary, finally a gleaming collection of letters—and you—have won absolute prestige: death. Useful for saying nothing, now you are in the timeless. Was that a victory? Underwear, sweat, shoes, tears—wherever you blow your nose—will not prevent the void from isolating you. If these were mythological tales, the analogy of yours would have dehumanized that melancholy lout crouching on his bed. Clean out your nostrils, look at the snot with amaze-ment, flick it or eat it, your gesture will not be linked to what fol-lows. But what, then, is the quality of this child I am killing, this delicious whore, whose everyday activities have the force and grav-ity of old myths?

They—or you yourself—do not forgive your beauty. They— and you yourself—would only burst out laughing before the inex-

tricable curses that overwhelm you. You will soon be nothing but
the memory of your beauty. The song of it will survive, then the
song of this poem that you desert, and further on, perhaps, "the
idea of infinite misery." Work. Brilliantly manifest what the world
has already condemned in you, not the stars. Give the whore you
are the coldest semblance. Taken from your shame, the wildest
earthly fineries will adorn your person. But who, what demon—
or you—is so bent on demolishing you? Destitution, tuberculosis,
prostitution, that hairy spot on your thigh!—and soon your blind-
ness, are your undoing. You, whose beauty is famous in Rome,
who persist in making yourself and unmaking yourself by cough-
ing up a fate so carefully planned that here you are, cut down to
suburban scale, one of the inimitable princesses of the great Greek
dynasties?

From what is the fabled camellia protecting you? Steam is worth
nothing to your delicate, flowery bronchial tubes. Feet bare on the
tiles, dressed in a terrycloth towel, in the condensation that, along
with shame, pushes you back and cuts you off, you could have
offered your golden rump. Rump presented to old men's dicks.
Your inner collapse held you back at the door. What a dream for
your pride, you, the most desired one—without knowing the ones
in Rome, I watch you in the Turkish baths where you thought of
prostituting yourself—waited for, offered, conqueror, infernal
among those oily and wounding bodies, traveling through silence
and illuminating it by: your teeth, your eyes, your cynicism, that
mass of white, sweaty steam.

For them—tuberculosis and death—here is my remedy: you are
a whore. The *word* is not a title, it tells your profession. Be a sublime whore. You recite—as the poetic language entirely within you
turns toward death where you are lazily burying yourself—with a
high, expressionless voice an erased text. What will die when you
die will be not a man, but a herald, bearing depleted coats of arms.

Nocturnal! These unusable words that want to disembody you, then transform you into a vague, uncertain, yet real product of language, they are not brought in just by whim: you are nocturnal,[2] sick, and false; never wondering at daylight, the rational, and your eye is astonished. Lucid, the beginning of this letter placed you in a vaporous element that your material substance cuts and shapes, but in which you participate, in which dreamily you take refuge. Never next to or facing the other, you enter him if you aren't already wrapped round him. He inhales you and vomits, or you suck him in and in your white belly, swallowed, he sleeps in a ball.

Certain emblematic characteristics will illustrate you: your illness. You are dying from your chest. Rottenness lives in this place, which without it would have been deserted. Here, to define you, are some insidious suggestions: a cough will carry you off, have one foot in the grave, vomit your lungs, spit oysters . . . terrific! This masterpiece of grace, this david, this perseus who walk, who move their heads, who climb a staircase, who button up their flies, who soap themselves and paint themselves, they were rotting. The exceptional light of the translucent cartilage of your nose shows that this admirable appearance is decomposing. Stopping your skin from being proud and vain, sickness forces it to meditation, to sadness, to grief. Tuberculosis makes you live. It is a giant bacillus that makes you distinctive with ...

... hide, moss, lichen, traces of the monster! Covered with a too-smooth fur that does not belong to your body, but to the animal of which it is the last visible trace that you preserve, a stain almost purple, plated on your thigh, gives your beauty the unique seal. It makes your perfection shameful, but especially when your hand by mistake rests on it—or your lovers' gaze—it hurls you into a solitary Antiquity, shadowy and mocking. You, a smile a challenge and anxiety then on your mouth: red alert!

## The Pretext

The thought—not the summons—but the thought of suicide, appeared to me clearly around my fortieth year, brought, it seems to me, by the boredom of living, by an inner void that nothing, except an absolute decline, seemed able to abolish. Still, no vertigo, no dramatic or violent impulse propelled me toward death. I calmly considered the idea, with a little horror, nauseous potion, and nothing more. At the time, after some wretched affairs undergone and then transformed into songs from which I tried to extract a particular morality,[3] I no longer had the vigor (though I felt the innermost urgency) to undertake a work that came not from fact, but from clear reason, a calculated work that came paradoxically from number before having come from the word, from the word before the deed, undoing itself as it unfolded. This weird demand was then illustrated by this formula: to sculpt a stone into the form of a stone. For reasons I will give, hardly interested in the world's fate, having (or believing I had) accomplished my own, by my inner void condemned to silence—sculpting a stone in the form of a stone the same as being silent—logically and naturally I contemplated suicide. What exists, existing, the powers of poetry, seemed vain to me: I had to disappear. Or exhaust myself in a long moment—until my natural death—in contemplation of the one I had become. Or mask my boredom beneath vanities.

Homosexuality is not a given that I could get used to. Beside the fact that no tradition comes to the aid of the pederast, or bequeaths him a system of references—except by omissions—or teaches him a moral convention having to do with homosexuality alone, this very nature, acquired or given, is experienced as a topic of guilt. It isolates me, cuts me off both from the rest of the world and from every pederast. We hate each other, within ourselves and within each of us. We destroy each other. Our relationships broken, inversion is lived solitarily. Language, that support endlessly reborn from a link between men—pederasts change it, parody it, dissolve it. Among themselves, freed from the severe social gaze, these queens recognize each other in the shame that they dress in faded finery. Reality[4] loses ground and lets a tragic insecurity appear.

   To die on the field of honor, your carnivals, Queers, have this extravagant allure: bugles, flags, and to croak riddled with shrapnel to save France. This long, declamatory suicide will never end, except death in the form of heroism, in order to return from that distant exile where woman is absent. But wars are rare. So, patiently, you will wait for a deed you can perform to restore you to the Fable: abstract universe, where you will be a symbol. Truly, in the massacre of Chaeronea [the massacre of the "Sacred Band" of young Theban warriors during Philip of Macedon's defeat of Athens—*Trans.*], could we see anything but an enormous suicide? Still, when the wish to quit life through the sign becomes urgent, patiently observe in yourselves what long, tragic cries call you. But—feathers, petticoats, eyelashes fluttering, fans—it is a funereal, but frivolous carnival that burdens you. Where can you take those rigors that order the themes, overcome them, write the poem? Where, finally, are the great tragic themes? Queers, you are made of pieces. Your gestures are broken. Do you expect a bullet finally to freeze you on the field of honor, so that you might be allowed, monstrously, to live through the metamorphosis for a few seconds?

   In the heart of a living and continuous system that contains us, that stumbles on reality and changes it, no pederast can be intelligent. Like their voice on certain words, their reasoning drifts or breaks. Now the notion of rupture appears.
   Pederasty comprises its own erotic system, its sensibility, its passions, its love, its ceremonial, its rites, its weddings, its mourning rituals, its songs: a civilization, but one that, instead of connecting, isolates, and that is lived solitarily in each of us. Finally, it is defunct. Accumulating, as it develops, gestures and considerations perverted by notions of rupture, of limits, of discontinuity, it constructs only apparent tombs. So I am going to try to isolate one of those dead civilizations from its living and continuous context. I will present it as purified as possible from all life.[5] Of this Egypt that is sinking little by little into the sand, futile and

grave, they will discover only a few fragments of tomb, a fragment of inscription.


But first let us kill the adolescent in us, then stifle the other. His
aim, outside of the criminal, crime certainly causes a death, in the
soul of its perpetrator it works its ravages, this act, alas, scarcely finished, fades away: it only passed by. When the victim is cold, does the
crime cease, or live on in rage, remorse, scenes, eternal, glimmering
regrets. Then let a sterile act revive an appearance, eternally cold and
sterile. May the crime never stop being accomplished. His tale is not
enough. The criminal turns within. He proceeds to his own expiato-
ry murder of himself. Starting from the crime—rupture—he develops
a rigorous logic and discovers laws, rules, and numbers that lead him
to the poem—the final sterile act that does not end by being performed. If our first crime was to refuse life and banish Woman, I will
track down in myself the child of whom I will speak—whom I sing,
dissect, and disembody—I will finish him off until the poem appears.
Not so this fairy will hate me, but so that my destination, after this
first crime, can be to perpetuate him according to rule and measure.


A civilization with its characteristics would have its own morality, if we call "morality" the lucid, voluntary attempt to coordi-
nate, then harmonize the scattered elements in the individual for
a goal that transcends him. But mine could not be ordinary morality. Pederasty is evil. To come to terms with it completely, inversion comprises, logically, the idea of sterility. The homosexual
refuses the woman who, ironically, takes revenge by reappearing in
him in order to put him in a risky position. They call us "effemi-
nate." Banished, sequestered, deceived, Woman, in our gestures
and intonations, seeks to be seen in daylight, and finds it: our
body, holed from the start, becomes unreal. It is no longer in its
place in the universe of the couple. The condemnation directed at
thieves and murderers is remissible, ours is not. They are guilty by
accident, our sin is original. We will pay dearly for the stupid pride
that makes us forget that we come from a placenta. For what
damns us—and damns all passion—is less our unfertile loves

than the sterile principle that fertilizes our acts, the least of our deeds, with nothingness. And so? Is it possible that my erotic frenzies constantly turned on myself or on the granite my lovers are, that these frenzies whose aim is my pleasure alone, accompany an order, a morality, a logic linked to an erotics leading to Love? I have hunted woman. Given this childlike and sulky attitude, I will pursue her with a coherent rigor. True, I refuse my tenderness to half the world, I refuse to follow the order of the world, innocently and clumsily I clear off: it will be solitude. Sterility will rise up and be constituted as action.

The end will be luxurious, the means wretched. With meticulous care in which no fragment of a second is spared, my mortal progress is carried on. This care—it is really our uninterrupted impatience with regard to the fierce lover whom his tuberculosis, helped by us, illuminates and kills. Everything will end with the dissolution of the one whom, unable to reach in his person, I will contain. Glory: to erect a tomb that will never exist, will never have existed, will enclose nothing. But to build it, and above all, secretly, and with great ceremony,[6] with a fierce hand to discover or reveal its pretext: a corpse.

The visible enterprise of every man is composed of acts that break the law. From any life, what remains? Its poem. At most a sign: the name become exemplary. In turn, the name and the example vanish, and "an idea of infinite misery" remains. Beyond its consoling and definitive harmony, this formula has this power: it completes me in what composes me. Thus explored by two bare feet that raise a wretched dust, if my glory were not this dust, this misery, these bloody feet, then what, what gold?

This singular dying man I am keeping alive—about whom I am speaking to you—watches over the caverns pitting his lungs. Caverns—that a pneumothorax is supposed to reduce—this word, with caution and silence leads me into grottos that conceal—treasure, dragon, apparitions of Mary, chimera or lily—nothing. Except my terror in discovering there, natural guest of these cavities, my invalid busily dying tenderly.

Each act wants to be sumptuous. Its idea is loaded with pomp. The essence of the means is misery. Each minute glory completing each act full of misery, the self of words is a death. Wanting to be written, memorable, each act is historic—whether it wants to be inscribed in one single, short memory or in many. The deed that breaks the law has a power of writing.

It is a profound misery, so dense that it sparkles, is actualized, and is called here beauty or glory. That is the idea of infinite misery that I want to rediscover. If it is the very essence of glory, may this idea alone remain attached to my name. May my name disappear, and may there remain this single idea of infinite misery.

If it is true that each work is pursued and completed according to a rigor that refers to nothing but a constant fidelity in its relationships, thus in a life that, comparable to the work of art, is rupture and end in itself, all morality is only coherent order referring to nothing but a constant fidelity in the relationship of actions between themselves. Queens, our morality was an aesthetics.

From every one of us, Woman—and whatever love, continuity, hope her approach contains—will be absent.[7] I will be dry, mineral, abstract. Let's have a shot at it. So, during this dying existence, in which constantly appearing death countered constantly by thought then by the action born from thought, during this existence paradoxically composed of sterile acts, if between them and the funereal principle that orders them I realize a strict correlation, perhaps, by these relationships alone I will realize a logic having its own laws and meaning: as rigorous as the logic in which the principle of love is contained. If I succeed, I will have won a curious virility. Alone, like an extinct civilization, my meaning *will speak* as equal to equal with the world where we are in the world, with that universe that perpetuates itself. Alone already, solitary, I consider it from the bottom of a well, refracted. It is no longer made for me. What fatal event, clumsy and cruel, from my childhood on—my tender childhood—made me thus steer clear of life? Incapable of an act that would have freed me from it, I chose this symbolic, but imperfect death. I should have died. Since then, I keep myself in suspense between death and life. That is the meaning of our ambiguity: we couldn't decide in favor of either one of them.

So I had undertaken to suffer pederasty, that is to say, guilt in its complete demand, by treating it with rigor, trying to discover its elements and its consequences, all of them come from evil, antisocial obsessions. From the pederastic given radiated a complex, imaginary crime—betrayal—that I tried to live, to actualize in myself with the greatest severity, in short, to transmute into a moral attitude, although I was living in a universe that imposed laws on me—from which laws I was borrowing a simulated security, to control myself—drawn from a complex resulting from the idea of continuity. Drawn to that traditional totality that condemned me and from which I had proudly excluded myself, my attitude was false and painful (inside this living organism, my pride had not magnificently isolated me so I could be the chief, or the only one: it is the organism that exiled me. Pride changed the exile into voluntary refusal, but the luminous, endlessly desired solitude of the artist is the opposite of the dismal and arrogant reclusion of pederasts).

Strange mistake: a young lower-class boy had a face in which I thought I read the adventures we attribute to criminals. His beauty hooked me. I linked up to him, hoping to relive in him a passion outside the law. But he was solar, in harmony with the order of the world. When I saw this, it was too late, I loved him. Helping him to realize himself in himself and not in me,[8] little by little, subtly, the order of the world was to change my morality. Still, helping this child in his effort to live in the world harmoniously, I did not abandon the idea of a satanic morality that, no longer lived according to a passionate cynicism, became an artificial, antique notion. Lucid again, I knew myself in confusion and comfort. Resolving, through a calm insolence, through the calm assertion of myself, the social scandal provoked by pederasty, I thought I was free of it with regard to the world and to myself. I was weary, even though the anxiety of eternity rose up, tormenting, an anxiety incapable of being translated in my case through the sequence of generations, or by the idea of continuity filling my acts, an anxiety I expressed by my search for a rhythm—or a law within my system alone—or a Golden Section, eternal, that is to say, capable of engendering, connecting, and completing the finished poem, perfect obvious sign, untouchable and final in this human affair, my own. I was in that state. In April 1952, in X . . . I met a twenty-year-old hoodlum. I fell in love with him. This country was then, and no doubt still is, an immense brothel where the pederasts of the whole world rented for an hour, for the night, or for the time of a journey, a boy or a man. Mine seemed at once delicate and precious. Neither his strangeness nor his beauty was obvious to me at first. His features seemed as if powdered with talc. At our second meeting, through a provocative sort of game on my side, by way of challenge, I expressed my disgust for his profession. Irritated, he offered to leave me. I accepted. He wanted to leave, stayed, left: I was in love. Magnetized, he led me on by the effect of a force whose nature I can only poorly define if it is in him, but if this appearance of power is only the appearance of my desire trussed, chewed, swallowed, shit out, I don't understand it any better, at least the poem doesn't help me to. I persisted in my desire for him. He was terrible, the lout I wanted to turn into an ornament with a hard-on, with open ass, and at the same time a friend. He fought against me.

Let them bring me a corpse. Tuberculosis is a disease of slow progression. But certain. The hero responsible for this infernal debauchery seems not to contain it, but to bathe in it, in a subtle element that reduces him to the point of annihilation. It is not so that he'll live and survive that I help my lover; it is so that he croaks. My attitude will be the demonstration that an act of ours ends, is devoured, refuses to engender the next one. I pursue my death and his own. Wherever he is, under whatever roof, may a fine rain pierce him to the marrow, ravage him, but above all, may a subtle despair blur his thoughts and cut him away from any plan. He will know he is dying. Geographic distance separates us, but we will individually pursue the same death-agony. Tragic imitation of the death his microbes and his ghosts are preparing for him, mine is also real. Reflection of the other, more affected, but more painful, it knows it is a comedy that can stop, but that—strict poem that it is—nothing will interrupt except the borders required by the order of the poem. The entire drama here will be the echo of a despair that is lived elsewhere, but elsewhere will be reflected in the echo that will come back to me. Reflection—reflecting—reflectiveness of the two suicides in slow motion that devour each other, that feed on each other and are exhausted in each other, this book also runs to its downfall, and to my own. No doubt it was a matter of the Lady of the Camellias, but in order to destroy: this Lady, her flesh, her clothes, her symbolic flowers, her name, my love, myself, up to the memory of all of that.

The most frivolous opinion, that death doubles each event, had sensed it already. Each gesture is woven from it. Knowing as inevitable the flight of everything from everything, we pursue the mistake itself. My adventure will be funereal in that every act is resolutely lived and thought not so it will engender the act that comes, but so that it will be reflected in itself, burst forth, explode, and win the most rigorous definition of itself, all the way to its annihilation. That is: the catafalque where there is no Emperor of Germany, on which a simulacrum is constructed, hollow ceremony, brief—or long—in honor of the whole absence.

Is this just a question of a simple anecdote reducible to: a pederast becomes infatuated with a young boy who deceives him? The pederast grieves, becomes enraged, hides. Ironic and sovereign, the child thinks he is strong. He fools and is fooled. He is subtle and cruel out of indifference. Those are the simple givens. The game is banal and easy.

Before knowing him, I had wanted to commit suicide. But his presence, and then his image in me, then his possible fate, coming not from him but from that image, overwhelmed me. He refused to exist according to this image. This unhappy passion soon took on an allure of catastrophe that, dizzily, could have led me to who knows what sterile act: suicide, murder, or madness.[9] I came through it for the poem. But I seem to have lived through miseries of such a baseness that I think I am coming back up from purgatory. Suicide? Hesitating between life and death, suspended in the void, awakened-asleep, I was working in sin on this hypocrite, vain death. You know? Before I knew that sick kid I had wanted to suppress myself: he is the one, that precious and savage dying one, who will become my blundered death. But why did such a fate take off from this image of him? But why, then, such an image, arising from his face and his body?

While an entertaining concern to live on the surface of the world—or, alive, to connect with the meaning of an obsession that feeds me and devours me?—suggested I raise a bloodless fairy to the stature of a thief,[10] my failure, subtly assented to, makes me modify this adventure, solve it according to inner givens, use it according to this funeral chant—secretly in harmony with the song of the thief— that will free me from it and from me in favor of the poem. It is my own destruction I am attempting, insofar as my language destroys the hero—who will die soon as a flesh and blood adolescent, but will pursue, as mythological principle, an infernal existence. Blind, a snake moves in the basalt. Him? That he lives and dies in a precise place in the world matters little. He must rot, and his rotting must make language stink and fail.

Finally this adventure that, on the level of anecdotal fact, will be a failure at once wished for and compelled, changes into a logical pursuit that is opposed to the morality of the world, and although it tries to deny it, it borrows from it all its notions, its terms of comparison—which are copious—in order to empty them. It seeks to build a spectral civilization, but doesn't know how to use words other than those that reflect a full and continuous reality. Finally, there's an even more laughable contradiction: this system that it wants to elaborate and make coherent, that is to say, capable of facing the world, it is hatred, not love, that will have to set the measure of its inner relationships, but hatred does not connect, it isolates. Let us try.

## Fragments of a Second Discourse

Beneath your glacial appearance, what shiver could move you?

—What's wrong?
—Nothing
—Yes
—Nothing
—You're sad
—So I'm sad
—Why
—Because I'm sad
—Why sad
—Because

What steps, carved out of hard appearance, go down backward, Shades? What preparatory simulacrum to start with? Under a clear, cold light, enter, the rooms are ready: on the facing walls, the mirrors do not multiply the play of the event, but are a prelude to its absence.

These round silences have the shape of your head, so I break them with a quick blow so that out come

One single—close to mine that grazes it—one single sex? Thousands against thousands who are mine who am thousands—move, stand still, kick gently, in these implacable mirrors, impenetrable, where the law of silence is absolute.

A thousand times the other is repeated, his cough comes out a thousand times invisible from a thousand times his gaping mouth and—except for one close to mine—a thousand times deaf and a thousand times I expire at being unable to reduce the universe to this immobile, brutal, and insane reflection!

Guards, invisible, but knowing, Fortunately guard the enclosed image. Never will it come ...

—Nothing
—But why?
—I'm sad
—Yes?
—Because

—Why sad?
—My friend doesn't have
a suit
—Why
—He gave it
Your eye aims at life
—He gave it? To whom?
—To a dead man.

If only I were outside the room
so I could see myself seeing myself
in it!

Beneath the stream a thousand
times gushing up—in the mirrors
and the gilded frames—urine and
its steam, of an Other, indispen-
sable, but always interchangeable,
thighs dripping, but confident,
torso, neck, belly too—a hand—
a thousand hands—when the
other blends in—a thousand others blend into Absence—holds a
mirror!
    Let's go on. A thousand times
the other's hand on a thousand
times my neck. A thousand
times—infinitely I move, infinitely
I change angles, infinitely I am
broken. . . . Cut! in the space finally abolished by the frost. . . . No.
The mirror room is extinguished.
Empty?

So one of yours could be properly buried, his friend offered his
only suit, and the young people made fun of him: you fought with
them. There exists, then, and you know it, above the reason of the
practical, a reason that requires you to strip yourself to wrap some
stinking meat: it is poetic reason, the one that thrusts away the
event and fixes it in the motionless sky of language. No doubt the
shameless, offending dead man was also handsome, freeing by
fracture another and scathing poetry, but it is you who just spoke
it, reduced to suburban scale—in Roman dialect, without being
careful about it—my tender Antigone.

The mythical camellia—now in heaven—that cruelly symbol-
ized you, has metamorphosed into you, fateful consumptive, consumptive vamp! Your glorious consumption. . . . Beat, drums! By
angles and mirrors, a villainous theater offers us a capital execution. Ironic, you climb three steps and come to win your periodic
resurrection. What crime, that the myth preserves, leads you to
your execution, offers you to the axe? Getting screwed, fucked,
frees you. From what? You lick the executioner, no, you kiss him.
You oil him, arouse him, overcome him. You make him cry.


Phaedra, living queen, in love with Hippolytus, there is the
crime. Still she is sovereign and already out of reach, scandalous,
but let her die, accept seeing her projected on the sky, looking
with mortal eyes at her exiled passion offering itself to the world
as an example: everything is resolved.
  On your knees on the unmade bed, you offer your behind to
the executioner, but the image that sums up this instant, the
point of the body where your being precipitates, is your childlike
neck bent on the pillow. Is it its already withered fall or an invisible hand that pulls your hair in front and mixes it with your
drool, your tears, and your mucous? On your knees—but facing
what god or what monumental absence?—you are executed.
Become: a whore, then the sublime slut, the queen—you, faggot
of the bloody spittle, the goddess, a constellation, then the name
alone of that constellation, and that name a used-up sign that a
poet can use. But a whore first and dying every time. Croak, or,
for you alone, use your wretchedness. But facing this mysterious
nothingness, you kneel down: he slices your neck when a prick
sodomizes you. Mocking, your awakening is simple. Intact, smiling—and free—you walk down the platform on the executioner's
arm.
  Terrible shortened Mass just for you, leaning over—before this
solemn absence, but renewing itself by us, the Queers, Fairies, not
of birth, but of death, around your coffin twisting our bodies.

Long ago, your wretchedness, your consumption, that radiant evening, dazzled us.


This last page I want to mark with the insolent, invisible step of that cruel instant—but maybe it was still you, mocker, making fun of your next descent into hell? In front of you, or if not you, some other infernal and transparent demon come out of you as you came out of me, who dared to say that a well-cut woolen suit looks better on a svelte and mocking lout, winking, his hair ruffled by the wind, than on his corpse? Who? The invisible Unknown had your smile in his teeth when—undressing me, too, and sending me back to the tomb—you dared say to me: "My kisses? I was just teasing you."

Get up! Go die! Not for a delicious widowhood and then another wedding, it is your absolute death that I am trying for, and my own. At my disposal I had the usual means: poisons, fear (you were dead of fear when you got tiny coffins containing your disfigured image), bullets, crushing you under my car, smashing you on the rocks! With a clean blow, to kill this handsome child would not have kept his ghost from hating me and going on to animate an even more handsome body, and the irony of that would have finished me. A more subtle death is being prepared.

# § 5   Letter to Jean-Jacques Pauvert

My dear Pauvert,

So you need to have a spectacle. But what can I say of a play on which I turned my back even before it was finished? [This letter was first published as an introduction to the two versions of *Les bonnes*, which Pauvert published. — *Trans.*] To speak of its composition would be to evoke a world and a region without greatness. The reasons that allow you to edit both versions have become uninteresting to me. I will only indicate that the second one—the most talkative one—was in fact the first. Long rehearsals pruned it, simplified it. But I would rather say a few words about theater in general. I do not like it. Reading the play will convince you of this. What I have been told of Japanese, Chinese, or Balinese ceremonies, and perhaps the inflated image of them that persists in my brain, makes the format of Western theater too coarse to me. We can only dream of an art that would be a profound labyrinth of active symbols, able to speak to the public a language in which nothing would be said, but everything felt. But any poet who attempted this adventure would be confronted with the insolent stupidity of actors and theater people. If, rarely, their triviality subsides, then their lack of culture and stupidity appear. One can expect nothing from a livelihood that is exercised with such little gravity or contemplation. Its point of departure, its reason for being, is exhibitionism. Beginning with any kind of aberrant attitude, you can elaborate a moral code or an aesthetics—you need only courage and renunciation, and the actor's choice of livelihood is motivated by his mistaken idea that the world is not demanding, but easily pleased. The Western actor does not try to become a sign charged with signs; he just wants to identify with a tragic or comic character. The actual world, tired, unable to live in actions, leads him even more into this vulgarity by making him represent in its place not heroic themes, but dreamed-up characters. What could the morality of these people be, then? If they do not stagnate in intellectual, but bitter seediness, they work for top billing. Look at them fighting for the front page in the newspapers. So instead of founding a conservatory, we should found a sort of seminary, and then, starting from it, build theatrical constructions with all the texts, sets, gestures they must entail. For even the most beautiful Western plays have an air of chaos, of masquerade, not of ceremony. What unfolds on the set is always puerile. The beauty of the language sometimes deceives us as to the profundity of the theme. In the theater, everything happens in the visible world and nowhere else.

Commissioned by an actor who was famous in his day, my play was written, then, out of vanity, but in boredom. I abandon it to the publisher, in its two tentative versions, but may it remain a proof of inspired stupidity. Still—I am still speaking of its making—already moved by the dreary sadness of a theater that too exactly reflects the visible world, the actions of men, and not of gods, I tried to achieve a distancing that, allowing a declamatory tone, would devote the theater to theater. I thus hoped to obtain the abolition of characters—who usually seem true only because of psychological conventions—in favor of signs that were as far as possible from what they seemed at first to signify, but still linked together, so that, by this single link, the author and spectator could be united. In short, to manage it so that these characters were nothing on the set except the metaphor of what they should represent. To bring this off, I had, of course, also to invent a tone of voice, a walk, a gesture. . . . It is a failure. I accuse myself, then, of abandoning myself without courage to an undertaking without risks or dangers. But I repeat that I was encouraged to do it by this universe of the spectacle that is satisfied with approximation. The work of actors stems mostly from the teaching supplied in the official conservatories. Those who dared a few experiments were inspired by the East. Alas, they do it like ordinary women practicing yoga. The manners, customs, entourage of poets are often sadly frivolous, but what can be said of those of theater people? If a poet discovers a great theme and begins to give it order, he must, to complete it, imagine it played, but if he brings to his work the rigor, the patience, the investigations, the gravity with which one approaches a poem, if he discovers major themes and profound symbols, what actors would know how to express them?

Instead of contemplation, theater people live in the dispersion of themselves. Should they be blamed? Probably this profession imposes itself on them in this facile form because, beneath the eye of a well-fed and slightly jealous public, they lounge in a life that is short, but without danger, and in a mechanical apotheosis. I know marionettes would do the job better than they. Already we are thinking of using them. Still, it might nonetheless be possible that this theatrical formula that I summon, completely and uniquely allusive, is a personal taste of mine. Through this letter, I might be expressing nothing but my own mood.

On a stage almost the same as our own, on a dais, imagine recreating the end of a meal. Starting from this single elusive fact, the greatest modern drama has been expressed for two thousand years, every day, in the sacrifice of the Mass. The starting point disappears beneath the profusion of ornaments and symbols that still overwhelm us. Under the most familiar appearance—a crust of bread—we devour a god. Theatrically speaking, I know nothing more effective than the Elevation of the Host. When this *appearance appears* before us—but under what form, since all heads are bowed, the priest alone knows, perhaps it's God himself or a simple white wafer he holds at the tip of his four fingers?—or that other moment of the Mass when the priest, having broken up the

Host on the paten, to show the faithful—not the public!—the faithful? But they still lower their heads, they pray, too?—reconstitutes it and eats it. In his mouth, the Host cracks! A performance that does not act on my soul is vain. It is vain if I do not believe in what I see, which will stop—will never have been—as soon as the curtain falls. No doubt one of the functions of art is to substitute the effectiveness of beauty for religious faith. At least, this beauty must have the power of a poem, that is to say, of a crime. Let's go on.

I spoke of Communion. The modern theater is a diversion. It sometimes, rarely, happens that it is a diversion of quality. The word somehow evokes the idea of dispersion. I do not know any plays that unite the spectators, even for an hour. On the contrary, plays isolate them even more. Sartre told me, though, of having experienced this religious fervor during a theatrical performance: in a prisoner's camp, at Christmas, soldiers, mediocre actors, had put on a French play evoking some theme—revolt, captivity, courage?—and the distant Homeland was suddenly present not on the set, but in the room. A clandestine theater, to which one would come in secret, at night and masked, a theater in the catacombs, might still be possible. It would be enough to discover— or to create—the common Enemy, then the Homeland to preserve or find again. I do not know what the theater would be in a socialist world, I understand better what it would be with the Mau-Mau, but in the Western world, more and more affected by death and turned toward it, it can only refine in the "reflection" of the comedy of comedy, of the reflection of reflection that a ceremonial play could make exquisite and bring close to invisibility. If one has chosen to watch oneself die deliciously, one must rigorously seek out and arrange the symbols of death. Or choose to live and discover the Enemy. For me, the Enemy will never exist anywhere, no Homeland will exist, even an abstract or inner one. If I am moved, it will be by the nostalgic recollection of what there was. A theater of shadows alone would still touch me. A young writer told me of having seen in a public garden five or six little kids playing at war. Divided into two troops, they were preparing for attack. Night, they said, was coming. But it was noon in the sky. So they decided that one of them would be Night. The youngest and frailest, having become an element, was then the master of the Combat. "He" was Time, the Moment, the Ineluctable. From very far away, it seemed, he came, with the calm of a cycle, but burdened by twilight sadness and ceremony. As he approached, the others, the Men, became nervous, anxious. . . . But the child, in their opinion, came too soon. He was ahead of himself: of one common accord, the Troops and the Chiefs decided to suppress Night, who became once again a soldier in a troop. . . . It is starting from this formula alone that a theater could delight me.

# § 6   The Studio of Alberto Giacometti

Every man has probably experienced that sort of grief, if not terror, at seeing how the world and its history seem caught in an ineluctable movement, which keeps gaining momentum and which seems able to change, toward ever coarser ends, nothing but the visible manifestations of the world. This visible world is what it is, and our action on it cannot make it be otherwise. So we think nostalgically about a universe in which man, instead of acting so furiously on visible appearances, would be employed in ridding himself of them, not just by refusing to act upon them, but by stripping himself enough to discover that secret place in ourselves from which an entirely different human adventure might possibly begin. More precisely, a moral one, no doubt. But, after all, it is perhaps to that inhuman condition, to that ineluctable arrangement, that we owe our nostalgia for a civilization that would try to venture somewhere beyond the measurable. It is Giacometti's body of work that makes our universe even more unbearable to me, so much does it seem that this artist knew how to remove whatever impeded his gaze so he could discover what remains of man when the pretence is removed. But perhaps Giacometti also needed the inhuman condition that is imposed on us so that his nostalgia could become so great that it would give him the strength to succeed in his search. Whatever the case may be, his entire oeuvre seems to me to be this search and has to do not only

41

with man, but also with anything at all, with the most banal of objects. And when he succeeded in ridding the chosen object or being from its utilitarian pretence, the image he gives us of it is magnificent. Well-deserved if foreseeable reward.

Beauty has no other origin than a wound, unique, different for each person, hidden or visible, that everyone keeps in himself, that he preserves and to which he withdraws when he wants to leave the world for a temporary, but profound solitude. There's a big difference between this art and what we call "sordid realism" [misérabilisme]. Giacometti's art seems to me to want to discover that secret wound of every being, and even of every object, so that it can illumine them.

When there suddenly appeared—for the niche is cleanly cut, level with the wall—Osiris beneath the green light, I was afraid. My eyes, naturally, were the first to know? No. My shoulders first, and the nape of my neck that a hand was crushing, or a mass that compelled me to sink into the Egyptian millennia and, mentally, to bend down, and even more, to shrivel before this small statue with the hard gaze and smile. It was indeed a question of a god. Of the god of the inexorable. (I am speaking, perhaps you've already guessed, of the statue of Osiris, standing, in the crypt of the Louvre.) I was afraid because it was a question, without any possible doubt, of a god. Certain statues by Giacometti cause an emotion in me quite close to that terror, and a fascination almost as great.

They also cause this curious feeling in me: they are familiar, they walk in the street. And yet they are in the depths of time, at the origin of everything, they keep coming near and moving back, in a sovereign immobility. If my gaze tries to tame them, to approach them and—without fury, without anger or wrath, simply because of a distance between them and me that I had not noticed, so compressed and reduced was it, that made me think they were really close—they move out of sight: it is because this distance suddenly unfurled between them and me. Where do they go? While their image remains visible, where are they? (I am speaking especially of the eight great statues on exhibit this summer in Venice.) [Probably Giacometti's *Femmes de Venise*, exhibited in the 1956 Venice Biennale.—*Trans.*]

I don't quite understand what in art is called an innovator. Should a work be understood by future generations? But why? And what would that mean? That they could use it? For what purpose? I don't see it. But I understand better—though very obscurely—that every work of art, if it wants to reach the most spectacular proportions, must, with infinite patience and care from the moment of its production onward, come down through the millennia, reach if it can the immemorial night peopled with the dead, who will recognize themselves in this work.

No, no, the work of art is not destined for unborn generations. It is offered to the innumerable populace of the dead. Who recognize it. Or refuse it. But these dead of whom I spoke have never been alive. Or I am forgetting. They were alive enough to be forgotten, enough so that their life's function was to make them cross to that calm shore where they wait for a sign—one that comes from here—that they recognize.

Although present here, where are those figures of Giacometti of which I spoke, if not in death? From which they escape at each summons of our eyes to come close to us.

I say to Giacometti:

ME: One must have a strong stomach to have one of your statues in one's house.

HIM: Why?

I hesitate to answer. My sentence will piss him off.

ME: One of your statues in a room, and the room is a temple.
He seems a little disconcerted.
HIM: And you think that's good?
ME: I don't know. And you, do you think that's good?
  The shoulders, especially, and the chest of two of them have the
delicacy of a skeleton that, if you touch it, will crumble away. The
curve of the shoulder—the joint of the arm—is exquisite . . .
(excuse me, but) is exquisite with strength. I touch the shoulder
and close my eyes: I cannot describe the happiness of my fingers.
First of all, for the first time they touch bronze. Then, someone
strong guides them and reassures them.


  He speaks in a harsh way, he seems to take pleasure in choosing
the intonations and words that are closest to ordinary conversation. Like a barrel maker.
HIM: You have seen them in plaster. . . . Do you remember
them, in plaster?
ME: Yes.
HIM: Do you think they lose something, being in bronze?
ME: No. Not at all.
HIM: Do you think they gain something?
  I still hesitate here to utter the phrase that will best express my
feeling:
ME: This will piss you off again, but I have a strange feeling. I
wouldn't say they gain by it, but that the bronze is what has
gained. For the first time in its life, the bronze has won. Your
women—they are a victory of bronze. Over itself, perhaps.
HIM: It would have to be like that.


  He smiles. And all the wrinkled skin of his face begins to laugh.
Strangely. The eyes laugh, of course, but the forehead, too (his
entire person is the gray of his studio). Out of sympathy, perhaps,
he has taken on the color of dust. His teeth laugh—spaced apart
and gray, too—the wind passes through them.

He looks at one of his statues:

HIM: It's a little misshapen, isn't it?

He often says this word [*biscornu*]. He also is somewhat misshapen. He scratches his gray, tousled head. Annette has trimmed his hair. He pulls up his gray trousers that were drooping onto his shoes. He was laughing six seconds ago, but he has just touched a rough-hewn statue: for half a minute he will be wholly in the transition from his fingers to the mass of clay. I do not interest him at all.

On the subject of bronze. During a dinner, one of his friends, teasing, no doubt—who was it?—says to him:

—Frankly, could a normally constituted brain live in such a flat head?

Giacometti knew that a brain could not live in a bronze skull, even if it had the exact measurements of M. René Coty's [president of the French Republic from 1954 to 1959—*Trans.*]. And, since the head will be in bronze, and since it must live, and since the bronze must live, one must then. . . . It's clear, isn't it?

Giacometti still insists: his ideal is the little rubber fetish statues they sell to South Americans in the lobby of the Folies-Bergère.

HIM: When I'm walking down the street and I see some chick, far away and all dressed up, I just see a chick. When she's in the room and completely naked in front of me, I see a goddess.

ME: For me, a nude woman is a nude woman. That hardly impresses me. I am quite incapable of seeing her as a goddess. But I see your statues as you see nude chicks.

HIM: Do you think I succeed in showing them as I see them?

This afternoon we are in the studio. I notice two canvases—two heads—of an extraordinary acuity, they seem to be in the midst of walking, coming to meet me, never stopping this motion toward me, and from I can't tell what depths of the canvas that keep expressing this sharp face.

HIM: It's a beginning, right?

He questions my expression. Then, reassured:

HIM: I made them the other night. From memory. . . . I also made some sketches (*he hesitates*) . . . but they're no good. Do you want to see them?

I must have answered strangely, so stupefied was I by the question. In the four years that I've been regularly seeing him, this is the first time he has offered to show me one of his works. The rest of the time he sees to it—a little surprised—that I see and admire.

So he opens a box and takes out six drawings, four of which are especially admirable. One of the ones that touched me the least shows a person of very small stature, placed at the very bottom of an immense white sheet.

HIM: I'm not very happy with it, but it's the first time I've dared to do that.

Perhaps he means to say: Emphasize such a great white surface with the help of such a tiny person? or: Show that the proportions of a person resist the crushing attempt made by an enormous surface? Or ...

Whatever he wanted to attempt, his thought moves me, coming from a man who doesn't stop taking risks. This little person, here, is one of his victories. What must he have conquered, Giacometti, that was so threatening?


When previously I said "for the dead," it was so that that innumerable crowd finally gets to see what they could not see when they were alive, standing up in their bones. There must be an art—not fluid, but on the contrary, very hard—gifted with the strange power to penetrate that realm of death, perhaps to seep through the porous walls of the kingdom of shadows. The injustice—and our pain—would be too great if one single shade were deprived of the knowledge of a single one of us, and our victory would be poor indeed if it did not let us earn a future glory. To the people of the dead, Giacometti's work communicates the knowledge of the solitude of each being and each thing, and that this solitude is our surest glory.

A work of art cannot be approached—who ever thought it could?—like a person, like a living being, or like another natural phenomenon. The poem, the painting, the statue need to be examined with a certain number of qualities. But let us talk about the painting.

A living face does not give itself over so easily, but the effort to discover its significance is not too great. I think—I venture—I think it is important to isolate it. If my gaze makes it escape everything that surrounds it, if my gaze (my attention) prevents this face from being confused with the rest of the world and from escaping ad infinitum into ever vaguer meanings, outside of itself, and if, on the other hand, this solitude by which my gaze cuts it off from the rest of the world is won, it is its meaning alone that will flow and pour into that face—or that person, or that being, or that phenomenon.—I mean that knowledge of a face, if it is supposed to be aesthetic, must refuse to be historical.

To examine a painting, a greater effort and a more complex operation are necessary. It is in fact the painter—or the sculptor—who has carried out for us the operation described above. It is thus the solitude of the person or the object represented that is restored to us, and we, who look, in order to perceive it and be touched by it must have an experience of space—not of its continuity, but its discontinuity.

Each object creates its infinite space.

If I look at the painting, as I said, it appears to me in its absolute solitude of object as painting. But that is not what preoccupies me. Rather, it is what its canvas must represent. So it is at once the image that is on the canvas—and the actual object it represents that I want to grasp in their solitude. So I must first try to isolate in its significance the painting as material object (canvas, frame, etc.), so that it stops belonging to the immense family of painting (even if it means bringing it back to that later on), but so that the image on the canvas becomes linked to my experience of space, to my knowledge of the solitude of objects, beings, or events as I described it above.

Whoever has never been filled with wonder at this solitude will not know the beauty of painting. If he claims to, he is lying.

Each statue, clearly, is different. I know only the statues of women for which Annette posed, and the busts of Diego—and each goddess and that god—here I hesitate: if, before these women, I have the feeling of facing goddesses—goddesses and not the statue of a goddess—Diego's bust never reaches that height, never even now, it does not withdraw—to return at a terrible speed—to that distance of which I was speaking. It is rather the bust of a priest belonging to the very high clergy. Not a god. But each statue, so different, is always linked to the same high, somber family. Familiar and very close. Inaccessible.

> *Giacometti, to whom I am reading this text, asks me why, in my opinion, this difference of intensity between the statues of women and the busts of Diego.*
>
> ME: *Maybe—(I hesitate to answer for a long time) . . . maybe because, despite everything, woman seems to you naturally more far away . . . or else you want to make her withdraw ...*
>
> *Despite myself, without saying anything to him, I recall the image of the Mother, placed so high up, or, what do I know?*
>
> HIM: *Yes, maybe that's it.*
>
> *He continues reading—I, my fading thought—but he raises his head, takes his broken, dirty glasses off his nose.*
>
> HIM: *Maybe it's because the statues of Annette show the whole individual, while Diego is only his bust. He is cut. Thus conventional. And it's that convention that makes him less distant.*
>
> *His explanation seems true to me.*
>
> ME: *You're right. It "socializes" him.*
>
> *Tonight, as I write this note, I am less convinced by what he said to me, for I do not know how he would model the legs. Or rather the rest of the body, for in such a sculpture, each organ or member is at*

*that point of prolongation of all the others in order to form the indis-*
*soluble individual, so that it loses even its name. "This" arm cannot*
*be imagined without the body that continues it and signifies it to the*
*extreme (the body being the prolongation of the arm), and yet I*
*know no arm more intensely, more expressly arm than that one.*

This resemblance, it seems to me, is not due to the artist's
"style." It is because each figure has the same origin, no doubt nocturnal, but well placed in the world.

Where?

About four years ago, I was on the train. Opposite me in the
compartment, an appalling old man was sitting. Dirty, and, obviously, mean, as some of his remarks proved to me. Refusing to pursue an unfruitful conversation with him, I wanted to read, but
despite myself, I looked at the little old man: he was very ugly. His
gaze crossed, as they say, mine, and, although I no longer know if it
was short or drawn-out, I suddenly knew the painful—yes, painful
feeling that any man was exactly—sorry, but I want to emphasize
"exactly"—"worth" any other man. "Anyone at all," I told myself,
"can be loved beyond his ugliness, his stupidity, his meanness."

It was a gaze, drawn-out or quick, that was caught in my own
and that made me aware of that. And what causes a man to be
loved beyond his ugliness or his meanness allows one to love precisely those things, his ugliness and meanness. Do not misunder-
stand: it was not a question of a goodness coming from me, but of
a recognition. Giacometti's gaze saw that a long time ago, and he
restores it to us. I say what I feel: this connection revealed by his
figures seems to be that precious point at which the human being
is brought back to the most irreducible part of him: his solitude of
being exactly equivalent to every other human being.

If—Giacometti's figures being incorruptible—the accident is
annihilated, what then remains?

Giacometti's bronze dog is admirable. It was even more hand-

some when its strange substance—plaster, mixed with string or
twine—crumbled away. The curve, without marked articulation
and yet perceptible, of his front paw is so beautiful that it alone
decides the supple walk of the dog. For it strolls, sniffing, its muzzle resting on the ground. It is thin.

I had forgotten the admirable cat: in plaster, from muzzle to tip
of tail, almost horizontal and capable of passing through a mouse-
hole. Its rigid horizontality perfectly reproduced the shape a cat
keeps, even when it is curled up.

As I am surprised that there is an animal—it's the only one
among his figures:

HIM: It's me. One day I saw myself in the street like that. I was
the dog.

If it was first chosen as a sign of misery and solitude, it seems to
me that this dog is drawn as a harmonious signature, the curve of
the spine answering the curve of the paw, but this signature is also
the supreme magnification of solitude.

This secret region, this solitude where beings—and things,
too—take refuge, it is this that gives so much beauty to the street;
for instance: I am in the bus, sitting there, I just have to look out.
The bus is hurtling downhill along the street. I'm going too fast to
be able to linger over a face or a gesture, my speed requires a cor-
responding speed from my gaze, so there isn't one face, one body,
one attitude prepared for me: they are naked. I note: a very tall,
very thin man, stooping, chest hollow, glasses and long nose; a fat
housewife walking slowly, heavily, sadly; an old man who is not a
handsome old man, a tree that is alone, next to a tree that is alone,
next to another . . . ; an office worker, another one, a multitude of
office workers, an entire city peopled with bent office workers,
wholly gathered into this detail of themselves that my gaze notes:
a fold of the mouth, a tiredness in the shoulders . . . each of their
attitudes, perhaps because of the speed of my gaze and of the vehi-
cle, is sketched so quickly, so quickly grasped in its arabesque, that
each being is revealed to me in its newest, most irreplaceable qual-

ity—and it's still a wound—thanks to the solitude where this wound places them, about which they know almost nothing, and yet into which their entire being flows. I thus cross a city sketched by Rembrandt, where each person and each thing is grasped in its truth, which leaves plastic beauty far behind. The city—made of solitude—would be the most perfect form of life, except that my bus passes some lovers crossing a square: they hold each other by the waist, and the girl has devised the charming gesture of placing her little hand in the hip pocket of the boy's jeans, so now this pretty and self-conscious gesture vulgarizes a page of masterpieces.

Solitude, as I understand it, does not mean a miserable condition, but rather a secret royalty, a profound incommunicability, but a more or less obscure knowledge of an unassailable singularity.

I cannot prevent myself from touching the statues: I turn away my eyes, and my hand continues its discoveries alone: the neck, the head, the nape of the neck, the shoulders. . . . Sensations flow to my fingertips. Not one that isn't different, so that my hand travels through an extremely varied and lively landscape.

FREDERICK II (*I think, listening, I think, to Mozart's* "Magic Flute"): Too many notes, too many notes!

—Sire, there isn't one too many.

My fingers remake what Giacometti's made, but while his sought support in wet plaster or clay, mine confidently put their steps back in his. And—finally!—my hand lives, my hand sees.

Their beauty—Giacometti's sculptures—seems to me to stem from the incessant, uninterrupted to-and-fro movement from the most extreme distance to the closest familiarity: this to-and-fro doesn't end, and that's how you can tell they are in movement.

We go have a drink. His is coffee. He stops to take better notice of the keen beauty of the Rue d'Alésia, such a light beauty, thanks to the locust trees, whose keen foliage, sharpened by transparency, in the sun more yellow than green, seems to suspend a gold powder above the street.

HIM: It's pretty, pretty ...

He resumes walking, limping. He tells me he was very happy when he found out that his operation—after an accident—would leave him lame. That is why I will chance this: his statues still give me the impression that they are taking refuge, finally, in some secret infirmity that grants them solitude.


Giacometti and I—and no doubt a few Parisians—know that there exists in Paris, where her home is, a person of great elegance, fine, haughty, sheer, singular, and gray—of a very tender gray: the Rue Oberkampf, which, casually, changes its name and calls itself higher up the Rue de Ménilmontant. Beautiful as a needle, it rises up to the sky. If one decides to traverse it by car, starting from the Boulevard Voltaire, as one climbs, it opens up, but in a curious way: instead of being farther apart, the houses come closer together, offering very simple façades and gables, of a great banality, but which, actually transfigured by the personality of this street, are flushed with a sort of goodness, familiar and faraway. Not long ago they put imbecilic little dark-blue discs on it, crossed by a red bar, supposed to indicate that parking is forbidden. Is the street spoiled, then? It is even more beautiful. Nothing—nothing!—could make it ugly.

How did it happen? Where did it dig up such a noble sweetness? How can it be at once so tender and so faraway, and how is it that one approaches it with respect? I hope Giacometti will pardon me, but it seems to me that this almost standing street is none other than one of his great statues, at once anxious, trembling, and serene.

It is not until the feet of the statues ...

A word here: except for the men walking, all Giacometti's statues have feet that look as if they were caught in one single, sloping block, very thick, that somewhat resembles a pedestal. From there, the body supports far off, high up, a minuscule head. This enormous—proportionally to the head—mass of plaster or bronze could make one think that these feet are charged with all the materiality of which the head rids itself . . . not at all; from these massive feet to the head an uninterrupted exchange takes place. These ladies do not wrench themselves out of a heavy mud: at twilight, they're going to slide down a slope drowned in shadow.

His statues seem to belong to a former time, to have been discovered after time and night—which worked on them with intelligence—had corroded them to give them that both sweet and hard feeling of *eternity that passes*. Or rather, they emerge from an oven, remnants of a terrible roasting: once the flames were extinguished, it had to remain that way.

But what flames!

Giacometti tells me that he once had the idea of molding a statue and burying it. (Immediately one thinks: "May the earth rest lightly on it.") Not so that it could be discovered by someone, even much later, when he himself and even the memory of his name have disappeared.

Would burying it be to offer it to the dead?

On the solitude of objects.

HIM: One day, in my room, I was looking at a napkin placed on a chair, and I actually had the impression that, not only was each object alone, but that it had a weight—or rather an absence of weight—that prevented it from weighing on another object. The napkin was alone, so alone that I had the impression of being able to lift the chair without the napkin changing place. It had its own place, its own weight, even its own silence. The world was light, light ...

If he had to give a present to someone he respected or loved, he might send her, certain of honoring her, gathered at the carpenter's, a curled shaving or a piece of birch bark.

His canvases. Seen in the studio (somewhat dark. Giacometti respects all substances to such a point that he would be angry if Annette destroyed the dust on the windows), for I can keep only a little distance, the portrait seems to me first like a tangle of curved lines, commas, closed circles crossed by a secant, mostly pink, gray, or black—a strange green is also mixed in—a very delicate tangle he was in the process of making, in which he no doubt lost himself. But I have the idea of taking the painting out into the courtyard: the result is frightening. As I move away (I will go so far as to open the door to the courtyard and go out into the street, retreating to sixty or seventy feet away) the face, with all its contours, appears to me, imposes itself—according to that already described phenomenon unique to Giacometti's figures—comes to meet me, swoops down on me, and hurries back into the canvas from which it came, becomes a terrible presence, reality, and form.

I said "its contours," but it is something else. For he never seems to be preoccupied with tones, or shadows, or conventional values. So he achieves a linear system that might only be drawings inside the drawing. But—and I don't really understand this—while he never sought contours with shadows or tones, or with the methods of any pictorial convention, somehow he achieves the most extraordinary depth. If I examine the canvas more closely, "contours" isn't right. It is rather a question of an unbreakable hardness the figure has obtained. It seems to have an extremely great molecular weight. It hasn't been brought to life, like some figures that are described as living because they were grasped in a particular instant of their movements, because they are shown by an accident that belongs to their history alone, but it is almost the opposite: the faces painted by Giacometti seem to have accumulated all life to the point that not one second more remains for them to live, or one gesture to make, and (not that they have just died) that they finally know death, for too much life is amassed in them. Seen sixty feet away, each portrait is a small mass of life, hard as a pebble, full as an egg, which could effortlessly feed a hundred other portraits.

---

As he paints: he refuses to establish a difference of "level"—or surface—between the different parts of the face. The same line, or the same ensemble of lines, can serve for the cheek, the eye, and the eyebrow. For him, eyes are not blue, cheeks pink, eyebrow black and curved: there is a continuous line that is made up of the cheek, the eye, and the eyebrow. There is no shadow of the nose on the cheek, or, rather, if it exists, this shadow must be treated as a part of the face, with the same traits, curves, valid here or there.

Placed in the midst of old bottles of solvent, his palette, in the final days: a puddle of mud of different grays.

This capacity to isolate an object and make its own, its unique significations flow into it is possible only through the historical abolition of the one who is looking. He must make an exceptional effort to divest himself of all history, so that he becomes not a sort of eternal present, but rather a vertiginous and uninterrupted passage from a past to a future, an oscillation of one extreme to another, preventing rest.

If I look at the armoire to know *finally* what it is, I eliminate all that is not it. And the effort I expend makes me a curious being: this being, this observer, stops being present, or even being a present observer: he continues to withdraw into an indefinite past and future. He stops being there so that the armoire can remain and so that between the armoire and him all emotional or utilitarian relationships are abolished.

(September '57.) The most beautiful statue by Giacometti—I'm speaking of three years ago—I discovered beneath the table, as I was bending down to pick up my cigarette butt. It was covered in dust, he was hiding it, a clumsy visitor's foot could have nicked it ...

HIM: If it's really strong, it will show itself, even if I hide it.

HIM: It's lovely! . . . it's *love*-ly! ...

In spite of his wishes to the contrary, he has preserved a little of the accent of the Grisons [Giacometti's home canton in Switzerland—*Trans.*]. . . . It's lovely! his eyes open wide, his smile is endearing; he was speaking of the dust covering all the old bottles of solvent that cluttered a table in the studio.

The bedroom, Annette's and his, is adorned with a pretty red-tiled floor. Previously, the floor had been stamped earth. It rained in the room. That is why, with a heavy heart, he resigned himself to the tiling. The prettiest, but humblest possible. He tells me that he will never have another dwelling besides this studio and bedroom. If it were possible, he would want them even more modest.

Lunching one day with Sartre, I repeat to him my saying on the statues: "It's the bronze that has gained."

"That is what could give him the greatest pleasure," Sartre tells me. "His dream would be to disappear completely behind his work. He would be even happier if the bronze, on its own, had manifested itself."

In order better to tame the work of art, I usually use this trick: I place myself, a little artificially, in a state of naivety; I speak of it—and to it, too—in the most ordinary way, I even babble a little. First I draw near. I speak to you of the noblest works—and I force myself to become more naïve and clumsy than I am. Thus I try to divest myself of my timidity.

"How funny that is . . . that's red . . . there's some red . . . and there's some blue . . . and you might say the painting was of mud ..."

The work loses a little of its solemnity. By means of a familiar recognition, I gently approach its secret. . . . With Giacometti's work, there's nothing to do. It is already too distant. Impossible to feign a nice stupidity. Sternly, it orders me to that solitary point from which it must be seen.

His drawings. He draws only with pen or hard pencil—the paper is often pitted, torn. The curves are hard, without softness, without gentleness. It seems to me that a line for him is a man: he treats it as an equal. Broken lines are sharp and give his drawing—thanks again to the granitic and paradoxically muffled substance of the pencil—a sparkling appearance. Diamonds. Diamonds all the more because of his way of using the white spaces. In the landscapes, for instance: the whole page could be a diamond of which one side is visible, thanks to broken and subtle lines, while the side on which the light falls—or, more precisely, from which the light would be reflected—will not let us see anything else but white. That makes for extraordinary jewels—one thinks of Cézanne's watercolors: thanks to these white spaces, where an invisible drawing can be implicitly understood, the sensation of space is obtained with a strength that makes this space almost measurable. (I was thinking especially of the interiors, with their suspended ceiling lights, and of the palm trees, but since then, he has made a series of four drawings representing a table in a vaulted hall that leave the ones I was recalling far behind.) Extraordinarily chiseled gems. And it's white—the white page—that Giacometti has chiseled.

About the four great drawings representing a table.
In certain canvases (Monet, Bonnard . . . ) air circulates. In the drawings I speak of, how can I say it . . . space circulates. Light, too. Without any of the conventional oppositions of value—shadow-light—light radiates, and a few lines sculpt it.

Giacometti's tussles with a Japanese face. The Japanese professor Yanaihara, whose portrait he was making, had to postpone his departure by two months, since Giacometti was never satisfied with the painting he began again every day. The professor returned to Japan without his portrait. This face without sharp edges, but serious and gentle, must have tried his genius. The paintings that survive are of an admirable intensity: a few gray, almost white lines on a gray, almost black background. And that same accumulation of life of which I spoke earlier. No way to make it hold anything else, not even one grain of life more. They are at that ultimate point where life resembles inanimate matter. Breathed faces.

I pose. He draws with precision—without artfully arranging them—the stove with its chimney, which are behind me. He knows he must be exact, faithful to the reality of objects.

HIM: One must make exactly what is in front of one.

I say yes. Then, after a moment of silence:

HIM: And, in addition, one must also make a painting.

He misses the brothels that have disappeared. I think they held—and their memory still holds—too much importance in his life for one not to speak of them. It seems to me he entered them almost as a worshipper. He came there to see himself on his knees opposite an implacable and distant divinity. Between each naked whore and him, there was perhaps this same distance that each of his statues keeps establishing between themselves and us. Each statue seems to withdraw into—or come from—a night so distant and dense that it is confused with death: thus each whore should return to a mysterious night where she was queen. And he, abandoned on a shore from which he sees her grow at once shorter and taller at the same time.

I'll risk this too: isn't it at the brothel that a woman can take pride in a wound that will never again free her from solitude, and isn't it the brothel that will rid her of any utilitarian purpose, thus making her win a sort of purity.

Many of his great statues are gilded.

During the entire time he struggled with Yanaihara's face (one can imagine the face offering itself and refusing to let its resemblance pass onto the canvas, as if it had to defend its unique identity), I had the moving spectacle of a man who never made a mistake, but who got lost all the time. He kept sinking into the distance, into impossible regions, without any way out. These days he has come back. His work is still at once darkened and dazzled by those regions. (The four great drawings of the table immediately follow that time.) Sartre tells me:

SARTRE: I saw him during the Japanese time, things weren't going well.

ME: He still says that. He is never happy.

SARTRE: Back then, he was really desperate.

About the drawings, I wrote: "Infinitely precious objects. . . ." I meant also that the white spaces give the page an Oriental quality—or one of light—the lines used not so that they take on a significant value, but with the sole purpose of giving all significance to the white spaces. The lines are there only to give form and solidity to the white spaces. Look carefully: it is not the line that is elegant, it is the white space contained by it. It is not the line that is full, it is the white space.

And why is that?

Maybe because besides the palm tree or the suspended ceiling lights—and the very particular space in which they are inscribed—that he wants to restore to us, Giacometti is trying to give a perceptible reality to what was only absence—or if you like, indeterminate uniformity—that is to say, the white space, and even, more profoundly, the sheet of paper. It seems, once again, that he has given himself the mission of ennobling a sheet of white paper that, without his lines, would never have existed.

Am I mistaken? That's possible.

But while he pinned the white sheet in front of him, I had the impression that he has as much respect and restraint faced with its

mystery as he does when faced with the object he is going to draw.
(I had already noted that his drawings recalled typography on
the page: [Mallarmé's] "A Throw of the Dice.")

The entire work of the sculptor and painter could be entitled,
"The invisible object."

Not only do the statues come straight up to you, as if they had
been very far away, from the depths of an extremely distant horizon, but wherever you are in relation to them, they arrange themselves so that you, who are looking at them, are at their feet. In the
very back of a distant horizon, they are on an eminence, and you
at the foot of the mound. They come, impatient to rejoin you and
to go beyond you.

For I keep coming back to those women, now in bronze (for the
most part gilded and patina'd): around them space vibrates.
Nothing is at rest anymore. It may be because each angle (made
with Giacometti's thumb when he was working the clay) or curve,
or bump, or ridge, or shattered tip of metal is itself not at rest.
Each of them continues to emit the sensibility that created them.
No point or edge that cuts, tears apart space, is dead.

The back of these women, though, is perhaps more human than
their front. The nape of the neck, the shoulders, the curve of the
haunch, the buttocks, seem to have been modeled more "amorous-
ly" than the entire front. Seen in three-quarter profile, this movement back and forth between woman and goddess is perhaps what
is most troubling. The emotion is sometimes unbearable.

For I could not prevent myself from coming back to that populace of gilded—and sometimes painted—sentries that, standing,
motionless, keep watch.

Next to them, how Rodin's statues or Maillol's are close to
belching, then falling asleep!

The statues (those women) of Giacometti keep watch over a dead man.

The man walking, spindly. His foot folded back. He will never stop. And he walks well and truly on earth, that is, on a sphere.

When it got around that Giacometti was doing my portrait (I would get a rather round, thick face) they told me: "He's going to make your head into a knife blade." The clay bust is still not finished, but I think I know why he used, for the different paintings, lines that seem to flee out from the median line of the face—nose, mouth, chin—toward the ears and, if possible, down to the neck. This is, it seems to me, because a face offers all the force of its significance when it is frontal, and everything must go from this center to nourish and fortify what is behind, hidden. I hate saying it so poorly, but I have the impression—as when one pulls one's hair back from the forehead and temples—that the painter pulls back (behind the canvas) the meaning of the face.

The busts of Diego *can* be seen from any vantage: three-quarters, profile, back . . . they *must* be seen from the front. The significance of the face—its profound resemblance—instead of accumulating on the face, flees away, sinks into the infinite, into a place never reached, behind the bust.

(It goes without saying that I am above all trying to pinpoint an emotion, to describe it, not to explain the artist's techniques.)

One of Giacometti's remarks, often repeated:
—You have to value [*il faut valoriser*] ...
I do not think he has ever once, one single time in his life, regarded a being or a thing with scorn. Everyone must appear to him in his most precious solitude.
HIM: I will never manage to put all the force there is in a head

into a portrait. The mere act of living already demands such a will and such energy ...

Faced with his statues, another feeling: these are all very beautiful people, but it seems to me that their sadness and solitude are comparable to the sadness and solitude of a deformed man who, suddenly naked, saw his deformation displayed, which at the same time he offered to the world in order to expose his solitude and glory. Which are unchangeable.

A few of Jouhandeau's characters have this naked majesty: Prudence Hautechaume.

Well-known and endlessly new joy of my fingers when I walk them—eyes closed—over a statue.

—No doubt, I tell myself, every bronze statue gives the same happiness to the fingers. At the house of friends who own two small statues, exact copies of Donatello, I want to recommence the experiment on them: the bronze no longer responds, mute, dead.

Giacometti, or the sculptor for the blind.

But ten years ago, I had already known the same pleasure when my hand, my fingers and palm, traveled over his floor lamps. It is indeed Giacometti's hands, not his eyes, that make his objects, his figures. He does not dream them, he experiences them.

He falls in love with his models. He loved the Japanese man.

His concern for the layout of a page seems to correspond to the feeling I indicated earlier: to ennoble the sheet of paper or the canvas.

At the café. While Giacometti is reading, a wretched, almost blind Arab causes a stir by calling one customer after another an asshole. . . . The insulted customer looks fixedly at the blind man,

angrily makes his jaw twitch, as if he were chewing his rage. The
Arab is thin, seems imbecilic. He bumps into an invisible, but
solid, wall. He understands nothing in the world where he is blind,
weak, and imbecilic, he swears at it in any of its manifestations.

—If you didn't have your white cane . . . ! shouts the Frenchman the Arab called an asshole. . . . I am secretly impressed that a
white cane can make this blind man holier than a king, stronger
than the most athletic butcher.

I offer the Arab a cigarette. His fingers look for it, find it a little by chance. He is small, thin, dirty, also a little drunk, stam-
mering, drooling. His beard is sparse and badly shaved. There
don't seem to be legs in his pants. So he scarcely keeps himself
upright. A wedding ring on his finger. I say a few words in his
language:

—You're married?

Giacometti continues his reading and I do not dare disturb
him. My attitude with the Arab annoys him, maybe.

—No . . . I don't have a wife.

As he tells me that, the Arab makes an up-and-down motion
with his hand to show me that he masturbates.

—No . . . no wife. . . . I have my hand . . . and with my hand . . .
no, there's nothing, nothing but my napkin . . . or the sheets ...

His white eyes, drained of color, sightless, are endlessly in
motion.

—and I will be punished . . . the good God will punish me . . .
you don't know everything I've done ...

Giacometti has finished his reading, he takes off his broken
glasses, puts them in his pocket, we go out. I'd like to comment
on the incident, but how would he respond, what would I say? I
know that he knows as well as I do that this wretched man preserves, maintains—along with his rages and furies—the point that
makes him identical to everyone and more precious than the rest
of the world: what survives when he steps back into himself, as far
as possible, as when the sea withdraws and abandons the shore.

I mentioned this anecdote because it seems to me that Giacometti's statues have withdrawn—abandoning the shore—to that

secret place, which I can neither describe nor clarify, but which causes each man, when he takes refuge in it, to be more precious than the rest of the world.

Well before that, Giacometti had told me of his amorous adventures with an old homeless woman, charming and in rags, probably dirty, and when she was entertaining him, he could see growths studding her almost bald skull.

HIM: I liked her, you know. When she didn't appear for two or three days, I went out into the street to see if she was coming. . . . She was worth all the beautiful women, wasn't she?

ME: You should've married her, and presented her as Mrs. Giacometti.

He looks at me, smiles a little:

HIM: You think so? If I'd done that, I would've cut a fine figure, wouldn't I?

ME: Yes.


There must be a connection between these severe, solitary figures and Giacometti's taste for whores. Thank God not everything is explainable, and I don't clearly see this connection, but I feel it. One day he tells me:

HIM: What I like about hookers is that they serve no purpose. They are there. That's all.

I do not think—I may be mistaken—that he ever painted one of them. If he had to, he would find himself faced with a being with its solitude to which another kind of solitude, which springs from despair, or vacuity, is added.


Strange feet or pedestals! I'll go back to them. Here it seems (at first sight, at least) that Giacometti observes—and I hope he'll forgive me—not just the demands of statuary and its laws (knowledge and reconstruction of space), but a private ritual according to which he will give the statue an authoritarian, landowner, feudal base. The effect of this base, on us, is magical . . . (they'll tell me that the whole figure is magical, yes, but the anxiety, the bewitchment that come to us from this fabulous clubfoot, is not the same as the rest. Frankly, I think here there is a rupture in Giacometti's craft: admirable in both ways, but opposite each other. With the head, the shoulders, the arms, the pelvis, he enlightens us. With the feet, he enchants us).

If he—Giacometti—could crush himself to powder, to dust, how happy he'd be!

—But the "chicks"?

It is hard for dust to win, to conquer the hearts of "chicks." He'd maybe nestle in the folds of their skin, so they could have a little dirt.

Since Giacometti allows me to choose—after a pause that didn't seem to have to end before my death or his own—I decide on a small head of me (here, a parenthesis) this head in fact is very small. Alone in the canvas, it measures no more than seven centimeters by three and a half or four, but it has the *strength, weight, and dimensions* of my actual head. When I take the painting out of the studio to look at it, I am disturbed, for I know I am as much in the canvas as facing it, looking at it—so I decide on this little head (full of life, and so heavy it seems like a small ball of iron during its trajectory).

HIM: Good, I'll give it to you. (*He looks at me.*) No kidding. It's yours. (*He looks at the canvas and says more vigorously, as if he were tearing out a nail:*) It's yours. You can take it away. . . . But later on . . . I have to add a piece of canvas to the bottom.

Now that he shows it to me, this correction does in fact seem necessary, but as much for the canvas itself that my little head shortens as for the head that thus takes on all its weight.

I am seated, very straight, immobile, rigid (if I move, he'll quickly bring me back to order, silence, and rest) on a very uncomfortable kitchen chair.

HIM, *looking at me wonderingly*: "How handsome you are!"—

He gives two or three brush strokes to the canvas without, it seems, ceasing to pierce me with his gaze. He murmurs again, as if to himself: "How handsome you are." Then he adds this observation, which amazes him even more: "Like everybody else, right? Neither more, nor less."

HIM: When I go for a walk, I never think of my work.

That may be true, but as soon as he enters his studio, he works. In a curious way, too. He is both striving for the realization of the statue—thus outside this place, outside all approach—and present. He doesn't stop sculpting.

Since these days the statues are very tall, standing in front of them—in brown clay—his fingers climb and descend like a gardener's trimming or grafting a climbing rose bush. The fingers play all along the statue. And it's the whole studio that vibrates and lives. I experience the curious impression that, if he is there, without his touching them, the old statues, already completed, are changed, transformed, because he works on one of their sisters. This studio, moreover, on the ground floor, will collapse at any given moment. It is made of worm-eaten wood, of gray powder, the statues are of plaster, showing string, oakum, or a tip of metal wire, the canvases, painted in gray, long ago lost the tranquility they had at the paint store, everything is stained and secondhand, everything is precarious and about to collapse, everything is ready to dissolve, everything floats: but all of that is as if seized in an absolute reality. When I have left the studio, when I'm in the street, then everything around me stops being real. Should I say it? In this studio, a man is slowly dying, is wasting away, and beneath our eyes is being metamorphosed into goddesses.

Giacometti does not work for his contemporaries or for future generations: he makes statues that finally delight the dead.

Did I say this already? Every object drawn or painted by Giacometti offers us, addresses us with, his friendliest, most affectionate thinking. Never does he appear in a disconcerting form, never does he want to seem a monster! On the contrary, from very far away he brings a sort of friendship and peace that are reassuring. Or, if they are disturbing, it is because they are so pure and rare. Being in harmony with such objects (apple, bottle, suspended ceiling light, table, palm tree) demands the rejection of all compromises.

I write that a kind of friendship shines from the objects, that they address us with a friendly thought. . . . That's exaggerating a little. Of Vermeer, that might be true. Giacometti is something else: it's not because it has made itself "more human"— because it's usable and endlessly used by man—that the object painted by Giacometti moves and reassures us, it's not because the best, kindest, most sensitive of human presences has handled it, but on the contrary, because it is "that object" in all its naïve freshness as object. Itself and nothing else. Itself in its total solitude.

I said that very badly, didn't I? Let's try again: it seems to me that in order to approach objects, Giacometti's eye, and then his pencil, strip themselves of all servile premeditation. On the pretext of ennobling it—or debasing it, according to the present fashion—he (Giacometti) refuses to impose on the object the tiniest human—be it delicate, cruel or strained—nuance.

Looking at a ceiling light, he says:

"It's a ceiling light, that's It." And nothing more.

And this sudden observation illuminates the painter. The ceiling light. On paper, it will exist in its most naïve bareness.

What a respect for objects. Each one has its beauty because it is "alone" in existing, there is the irreplaceable in it.

Giacometti's art is not, then, a social art because it establishes a social link—man and his secretions—between objects; it's rather an art of high-class tramps, so pure that what could unite them might be a recognition of the solitude of every being and every object. "I am alone," the object seems to say, "thus caught in a necessity against which you can do nothing. If I am nothing but what I am, I am indestructible. Being what I am, unreservedly, my solitude knows yours."

# § 7  The Tightrope Walker

*For Abdallah*

A gold sequin is a tiny disc of gilt metal, pierced with a hole. Thin and light, it can float on water. Sometimes one or two remain stuck in the curls of an acrobat.

This love—almost desperate, but charged with tenderness—that you must show for your wire, will have as much strength as the metal wire has to carry you. I know objects, their malignancy, their cruelty, their gratitude, too. The wire was dead—or if you like, mute, blind—but now that you are here, it will live and speak.

You will love it, with an almost carnal love. Each morning, before practice, when it is stretched out and vibrating, go give it a kiss. Ask it to support you, and that it grant you the elegance and nervousness of the hollow of the knee. At the end of the session, salute it, thank it. When it is still rolled up, at night, in its box, go see it, caress it. And, quietly, place your cheek against its own.

Some tamers use violence. You can try to tame your wire. Be careful. The metal wire, like the panther and like, they say, the public, loves blood. Win it over, instead.

A blacksmith—only a blacksmith with gray mustache and large shoulders can risk such delicacy—each morning he greeted his beloved, his anvil, thus:
—So, my beauty!
In the evening, the day over, his big paw would caress it. The anvil was not indifferent to this, and the blacksmith was aware of its feelings.

Give your metal wire the most beautiful expression, not of you, but of it. Your leaps, your somersaults, your dances—in acrobat slang, your pitter-patter, bows, midair somersaults, cartwheels, etc.—you will execute them successfully, not for you to shine, but so that a steel wire that was dead and voiceless will finally sing. How grateful it will be to you if you are perfect in your performance, not for your glory, but its own.
May the amazed audience applaud it:
—What a surprising wire! How it supports its dancer and how it loves him!
In its turn, the wire will be the most amazing dancer of you.

The ground will make you stumble.

Who before you ever understood what nostalgia rests enclosed in the soul of a seven-millimeter steel wire? And that it knew it was summoned to make a dancer leap with two turns in the air, with fouettés? Except for you, no one. Know its joy, then, and its gratitude.

I would not be surprised, when you walk on the earth, if you fall and sprain something. The wire will carry you better, more surely, than a road.

*Nonchalantly, I open his wallet and leaf through it. Among old photos, pay stubs, expired bus tickets, I find a folded piece of paper on which he has drawn curious signs: a straight line, which represents the wire, with slanting marks to the right and left—those are his feet, or rather the place his feet would take, it is the steps he will take. And opposite each mark, a number. Because he works to bring rigors, quantitative discipline, to an art that had been subject only to a haphazard and empirical training, he will conquer.*

*What do I care, then, if he knows how to read or not? He knows figures well enough to measure the rhythms and numbers. Clever with numbers, Joanovici was an illiterate Jew—or Gypsy. He earned a huge fortune during one of our wars by selling scrap metal.*

"A deadly solitude [*une solitude mortelle*] ..."
At the bar, you can crack jokes, drink with whomever you like, with anyone at all. But when the Angel is announced, stand alone to receive him. The Angel, for us, is evening, fallen on the dazzling arena. If your solitude, paradoxically, is spotlighted, and the darkness made up of thousands of eyes judging you, fearing and hoping for your fall, it matters little: you will dance on in a desert solitude, blindfolded, if you can, eyelids fastened shut. But nothing—especially not applause or laughter—will keep you from dancing for your image. You are an artist—alas—you can no longer deny yourself the monstrous precipice of your eyes. Narcissus dances? But it is something else besides vanity, egoism, and love of self that is at stake. Is it Death itself? Dance alone, then. Pale, livid, anxious to please or displease your image: but it is your image that will dance for you.

If your love, as well as your skill and cleverness, are great enough to reveal the secret possibilities of the wire, if the precision of your gestures is perfect, it will hurry to meet your foot (clothed in leather): it is not you who will dance, it is the wire. But if it is the wire that dances motionless, and if it is your image that it makes leap, where, then, will you be?

Death—the Death of which I speak to you—is not the one that will follow your fall, but the one that precedes your appearance on the wire. It is before climbing onto it that you die. The one who dances will be dead—bent on every beauty, capable of them all.

When you appear, a pallor—no, I am not speaking of fear, but of its opposite, of an invincible audacity—a pallor will cover you. Despite your makeup and your sequins, you will be pale, your soul livid. That is when your precision will be perfect. Since nothing more attaches you to the ground, you will be able to dance without falling. But be careful to die before appearing, so that a dead man dances on the wire.

*And your wound, where is it?*

*I wonder where it resides, where the secret wound is hidden where every man runs to take refuge if his pride is hurt, when he is wounded? This wound—which thus becomes the innermost core— it is this wound he will inflate, fill. Every man knows how to reach it, to the point of becoming this wound itself, a sort of secret, painful heart.*

*If we look, with a quick and greedy eye, at the man or woman[1] going by—or the dog, or bird, or jalopy—the very quickness of our gaze will reveal to us, neatly, what this wound is into which they withdraw when there is danger. What am I saying? They are there already, gaining through it—whose form they have taken—and for it, solitude: they exist entirely in the sluggishness of shoulder they pretend is themselves, their whole life flows into a mean fold of the mouth and against which they can do nothing, and want to do nothing, since it is through it that they know this absolute, incommunicable solitude—this castle of the soul—in order to be this solitude itself. For the tightrope walker of whom I speak, it is visible in his sad gaze, which has to reflect images of an unforgettably wretched childhood in which he knew he was abandoned.*

*It is into this wound—incurable, since it is himself—and into this solitude that he must throw himself, it is there he will be able to discover the strength, the audacity, and the skill necessary to his art.*

I ask you for a little attention. Look: to surrender yourself better to Death, to make it live in you with the most rigorous precision, you will have to keep yourself in perfect health. The least illness would restore you to our life. It would be broken, this block of absence that you are going to become. A sort of humidity with its patches of mildew would overcome you. Watch over your health.

*If I advise him to avoid luxury in his private life, if I advise him to be a little filthy, to wear shapeless clothes, worn-out shoes, it is so that, at night, in the arena, the change of scene may be greater, so that all the day's hope may find itself exalted by the approach of the show, so that from this very distance, from an apparent wretchedness to the most splendid apparition, would arise a tension such that the dance will be like a gunshot or a cry, it is because the reality of the Circus depends on this metamorphosis of dust into gold dust, but above all, it is because the one who has to revive this admirable image must be dead, or, if you prefer, must drag himself along the ground like the last, the most pitiful of humans. I would even go so far as to advise him to limp, to cover himself with rags, with lice, and to stink. His person should be more and more diminished to let this image of which I speak, inhabited by a dead man, sparkle ever more brilliantly. He should exist finally only in his appearance.*

It goes without saying that I did not mean to say that an acrobat who works eight or ten meters above ground must leave things to God (to the Virgin, tightrope walkers) and should pray and cross himself before entering the arena, for death is in the tent. As if to a poet, I was speaking to the artist alone. If you danced one meter above the carpet, my injunction would be the same. It is a question, you understand, of deadly solitude, of that desperate and brilliant region where the artist operates.

I will add, though, that you must risk an actual, physical death. The dramatic art of the Circus requires it. It is, along with poetry, war, and bullfighting, one of the only cruel games that remain. Danger has its reason: it will force your muscles to achieve a perfect precision—the least mistake would cause your fall, with injuries or death—and this precision will be the beauty of your dance. Reason thus: a blunderer on the wire does the midair somersault, he misses and kills himself, the audience is not too surprised, it was expecting it, it was almost hoping for it. You must know how to dance so beautifully, with such pure gestures, in order to seem precious and rare; thus, when you get ready to make the midair somersault, the public will be anxious, will be almost indignant that such a graceful being risks death. But you succeed in the somersault and return to the wire, while the spectators cheer you, for your skill consists in saving a very precious dancer from an indecent death.

*If he dreams, when he is alone, and if he dreams about himself, probably he sees himself in his glory, and no doubt he tried a hundred, a thousand times to grasp his future image: himself on the wire on a triumphant night. So he endeavors to represent himself to himself as he would like to be. And it is to this becoming what he would like to be, how he dreams himself, that he applies himself. Of course this dreamed-of image is far from what he will be on the actual wire. But that is what he seeks: later on to resemble this image of him that he invents for himself today. And so that, once he has appeared on the steel wire, there will remain in the audience's memory only an image identical to the one he invents for himself today. Curious project: to dream himself, to make this dream perceptible that will become a dream once again, in other heads!*

So it is frightening death, the frightening monster that lies in wait for you, that is conquered by the Death of which I told you.

Your makeup? Excessive. Extravagant. Make it elongate your eyes all the way to your hair. Your nails will be painted. Who, if he is normal and clear-headed, would walk on a wire or express himself in verse? It is too crazy. Man or woman? Definitely a monster. Rather than aggravate the singularity of such an exercise, makeup will lessen it: in fact, it makes more sense if it's an adorned, gilded, painted, finally equivocal being who walks there, without a balancing pole, where roofers or lawyers would never think of going.

Made-up, then, sumptuously, to the point of provoking nausea at the sight of him. During the first of your turns on the wire, they'll understand that this monster with mauve eyelids could dance nowhere but there. No doubt, they will tell themselves, it is this peculiarity that puts him on a wire, it is that elongated eye, those painted cheeks, those golden nails that force him to be there, where we—thank God!—will never go.

I am going to try to make myself understood better.

To acquire that absolute solitude he needs if he wants to complete his work—drawn from a nothingness that it will both fill in and make perceptible—the poet can put himself in danger in some posture that will be the riskiest for him. Cruelly, he repels any curious person, any friend, any appeal that might try to incline his work toward the world. If he likes, he can go about it this way: around him he leaves such a sickening, such a black smell that he finds himself lost in it, half-asphyxiated by it himself. People flee from him. He is alone. His seeming curse will allow him all daring innovations, since no gaze troubles him. He moves in an element that is like death, like the desert. His speech awakens no echo. Since it must utter what is addressed to no one and no longer has to be understood by anything that is living, it is a necessity that is not required by life, but by the death that commands him.

Solitude, I have told you, could be granted to you only by the presence of the audience, so you must go about it differently and have recourse to another procedure. Artificially, by an effect of your will, you should compel this imperviousness toward the world to enter you. As its waves mount up—like the coldness starting in Socrates' feet, making its way up to his legs, his thighs, his stomach—their coldness seizes your heart and freezes it.—No, no, again no, you are not there to amuse the public, but to fascinate it.

Confess that they would experience a curious impression—it would be astonishment, panic—if tonight they managed to behold a corpse walking on the high wire!

"Their coldness seizes your heart and freezes it . . ." but—and this is the most mysterious thing of all—a sort of steam must at the same time come from you, a light steam that does not blur your angles, letting us know that in your center, a hearth keeps feeding that glacial death that entered you through your feet.

And your costume? At once chaste and provocative. It is the skintight body stocking of the Circus, in blood-red jersey. It outlines your musculature exactly, it sheaths you, it gloves you, but from the collar—open in a circle, cut clean, as if the executioner were going to behead you tonight—from the collar to your hip, a sash, also red, but from which float tassels—fringed with gold. Red tennis shoes, sash, belt, collar's trim, ribbons under the knee, are embroidered with gold sequins. So that you sparkle, of course, but especially so that you lose in the sawdust, when you go from your dressing room to the arena, a few badly-sewn sequins, delicate symbols of the Circus. During the daytime, when you go to the grocer's, a few fall from your hair. Sweat has stuck one to your shoulder.

The bulge accentuated in the bodysuit, where your balls are enclosed, will be embroidered with a gold dragon.

*I tell him about Camilla Meyer—but I also want to tell him who that splendid Mexican was, Con Colléano, and how he danced!—Camilla Meyer was a German woman. When I saw her, she was about forty years old. In Marseille, she had set up her wire thirty meters above the pavement, in the courtyard of the Vieux-Port. It was night. Spotlights lit up the horizontal wire thirty meters high. To reach it, she climbed up on a slanting wire two hundred meters long that started at the ground. Arriving halfway up this slope, to rest, she put one knee on the wire, and kept the balancing-pole on her thigh. Her son (he was about sixteen), who was waiting for her on a little platform, brought a chair to the middle of the wire, and Camilla Meyer, who was coming from the other side, arrived on the horizontal wire. She took this chair, which rested on the wire with only two of its feet, and she sat down on it. Alone. She came down from it, alone. . . . Below, beneath her, all heads were lowered, hands hiding their eyes. Thus, the audience refused this politeness to the acrobat: to make the effort to look steadily at her when she brushes with death.*

*—And you, he said to me, what were you doing?*

*—I was watching. To help her, to salute her because she had led death to the edges of night, to accompany her in her fall and in her death.*

If you fall, you will deserve the most conventional funeral oration: puddle of gold and blood, pool where the setting sun. . . . You should expect nothing else. The circus is all convention.

For your entrance into the arena, avoid the pretentious walk. You enter: it is a series of leaps, of midair somersaults, of twirls, cartwheels, that bring you to the foot of your contrivance, onto which you climb, dancing. With your very first leap—begun in the wings—people should know already that they will go from wonder to wonder.

And dance!

But with a hard-on. Your body will have the arrogant vigor of a congested, irritated sex. That is why I advise you to dance in front of your image and to be in love with it. You can't get out of it: it is Narcissus who is dancing. But this dance is only your body's attempt to identify itself with your image as the spectator experiences it. You are no longer just mechanical and harmonious perfection: a wave of heat comes from you and warms us. Your stomach burns. Still, do not dance for us, but for you. It was not a whore we came to see at the Circus, but a solitary lover in pursuit of his image who saves himself and faints on a metal wire. And always in the infernal land. So it is this solitude that will fascinate us.

*Among other instants, the Spanish crowd awaits the one when the bull, with a thrust of his horn, will take the stitches out of the torero's pants: after the tear, the sex and blood. Stupidity of nudity that doesn't try to show or exalt a wound! So it is a body stocking the tightrope walker will have to wear, for he must be clothed. It will be illustrated: embroidered suns, stars, irises, birds . . . a body suit to protect the acrobat against the hardness of the public's gaze and so that an accident can be possible, so that one night, the body suit can give way, get torn.*

*Must it be said? I would want the tightrope walker to live during the day disguised as an old, toothless female tramp, with a gray wig: seeing her, one would know what athlete reposes beneath the rags, and one would respect such a great distance of day from night. To appear in the evening! And he, the tightrope walker, no longer knowing who his privileged self might be: the seedy female tramp, or the gleaming loner? Or the perpetual movement from her to him?*

Why dance tonight? Why leap, bound beneath the spotlights eight meters above the floor, on a wire? Because you must find yourself. Both game and hunter, tonight you flushed yourself out, you flee from yourself and hunt for yourself. Where were you, then, before entering the arena? Sadly dispersed in daily actions, you did not exist. Under its spotlights, you experience the necessity of order. Every night, for you alone, you will run on the wire, twist yourself on it, writhe on it in search of the harmonious being, scattered and lost in the thicket of your familiar gestures: tying your shoelace, blowing your nose, scratching yourself, buying soap. . . . But you only approach and grasp yourself for an instant. And always in that deadly, white solitude.

Your wire, though—I'll come back to it—do not forget that it is to its virtues that you owe your grace. To your own too, of course, but in order to discover and reveal its own. The game must be unbecoming to neither: play with it. Tease it with your toe, surprise it with your heel. Face one another, do not fear cruelty: sharp, it will make you sparkle. But always take care never to lose the most exquisite courtesy.

Know over whom you triumph. Over us, but . . . your dance will be hateful.

One is not an artist unless a great unhappiness is mixed in. Hatred against what god? And why conquer him?

The hunt on the wire, the pursuit of your image, and those arrows you riddle it with without touching it, and wound it and make it shine—it is a celebration. If you reach it, this image, it is the Celebration.

I am experiencing a strange thirst, I want to drink, that is to suffer, or to drink so that drunkenness comes from the suffering that a celebration would be. You wouldn't know how to be unhappy through illness, through hunger, through prison, since nothing forces you to be so, you have to be it through your art. What do we—you or I—care about a good acrobat: you will be that glowing wonder, you who burn, who last a few minutes. You burn. On your wire, you are lightning. Or if you like, a solitary dancer. Lit up by who knows what that illumines you, consumes you, it is a terrible misery that makes you dance. The audience? It sees nothing but fire, and, thinking you are playing, unaware that you are the arsonist, it applauds the fire.

Have a hard-on, and make others have one. This heat that comes from you and shines, it is your desire for yourself—or for your image—never satisfied.

Gothic legends [in fact, a short opera by Jules Massenet, *Le jongleur de Notre-Dame*, very popular in Genet's childhood, deals with this— *Trans.*] speak of street acrobats who, having nothing else, offered their tumbles to the Virgin. In front of the cathedral they danced. I do not know to what god you will address your games of skill, but you must have one. The one, perhaps, that you make exist for an hour and for the dance. Before your entrance in the arena, you were a man mingling with the throng in the wings. Nothing distinguished you from the other acrobats, jugglers, trapeze artists, horsewomen, stage hands, clowns.—Nothing, except that sadness already in your eyes, and do not chase it away, that would be to kick all poetry out of the door of your face!—God does not yet exist for anyone ... you arrange your dressing gown, you brush your teeth. .... Your gestures can be repeated ...

*Money? Dough? It must be earned. And until he dies of it, the tightrope walker must rake it in. .... One way or another, he will have to disorganize his life. That is when money can be useful, bringing a sort of rottenness that can pollute the calmest soul. A lot, a whole lot of dough! A load of it! A vile amount! And then to let it pile up in a corner of your shack, never touching it, wiping your ass with your finger. As night approaches, to wake up, tear yourself away from this evil, and in the evening, dance on the wire.*
    *I say to him again:*
    *—You will have to work to become famous ...*
    *—Why?*
    *—To hurt.*
    *—Do I have to earn so much dough?*
    *—You have to. On your metal wire you'll appear, and a rain of gold will shower down on you. But since nothing interests you but your dance, you will rot during the daytime.*
    *He should rot then in a way, a stench should crush him, sicken him, which fades away at the first trumpet call of evening.*

But you enter. If you dance for the public, it will know it, you'll be lost. There's one of your regulars. No longer fascinated by you, he'll sit heavily within himself, you'll never be able to tear him away from himself.

You enter, and you are alone. Seemingly, for God is there. He comes from I don't know where and perhaps you brought him when you entered, or solitude revives him, it's all the same. It is for him that you hunt your image. You dance. Face set. Gestures precise, bearing true. Impossible to repeat them, or you die for eternity. Severe and pale, dance, and, if you can, with your eyes closed.

Of what God am I speaking to you? I wonder. But he is absence of criticism and absolute judgment. He sees your quest. Either he accepts you and you sparkle, or he turns away. If you have chosen to dance before him alone, you cannot escape the precision of your articulate language, of which you become prisoner: you cannot fall.

Might God then be only the sum of all the possibilities of your will applied to your body on this metal wire? Divine possibilities!

When you practice, your midair somersault sometimes eludes you. Do not be afraid of considering your somersaults as so many rebellious animals that it is your job to tame. This somersault is within you, untamed, scattered—and thus unhappy. Do what you must to give it human form.

"A red body stocking with stars." I wanted the most traditional of costumes for you so that you could more easily wander into your image, and if you like, carry off your metal wire so that you both might finally disappear—but you can also, on this narrow path that comes from nowhere and goes nowhere—its six meters' length are an infinite line and a cage—give the performance of a tragedy.

And, who knows? If you fall off the wire? Stretcher bearers will carry you off. The orchestra will play. They'll bring in the tigers, or the horsewoman.

> *Like the theater, the circus takes place in the evening, as night approaches, but it can also be given in full daylight.*
> *If we go to the theater, it is to penetrate into the hall, into the anteroom of that precarious death that sleep will be. For it is a Celebration that will take place at close of day, the most serious one, the last one, something very close to our funeral. When the curtain rises, we enter a place where infernal replicas are being prepared. It is evening so that it can be pure (this celebration), so that it can unfold with no danger of being interrupted by a thought, by a practical requirement that could ruin it ...*
> · · · · · · · · · · · · · · · · · · · · · · ·
> *But the Circus! It needs keen, total attention.*
> *It is not our celebration that is presented. It is a game of skill that requires us to remain awake.*

The audience—which allows you to exist, without it you would never have the solitude I spoke about—the audience is the animal that you will finally stab. Your perfection, as well as your boldness, will, during the time you appear, annihilate it.

Rudeness of the audience: during your most dangerous movements, they will close their eyes. They close their eyes when in order to dazzle them you brush with death.

That brings me to say that one must love the Circus and despise the world. An enormous beast, brought back from diluvian times, places itself massively over the cities: we go in, and the monster is full of mechanical and cruel wonders: horsewomen, clowns, lions and their tamer, a magician, a juggler, German trapeze artists, a horse who speaks and counts, and you.

All of you are the remnants of a mythical age. You come from very far away. Your ancestors ate crushed glass, fire, they charmed serpents, doves, they juggled with eggs, they made a council of horses converse.

You are not ready for our world and its logic. So you must accept this misery: to live at night on the illusion of your mortal performances. During the day, you linger fearful at the circus door—not daring to enter our life—too firmly held back by the powers of the circus, which are the powers of death. Never leave this enormous canvas womb.

Outside is discordant noise, disorder: inside, it is the genealogical certainty that comes from millennia, the security of knowing one is connected in a sort of factory where precise rules are made that serve as the solemn exposition of yourselves, who prepare the Show. You live only for the Show. Not the one that fathers and mothers treat themselves to by paying. I'm speaking of your illumination of those few minutes. Obscurely, in the flanks of the monster, you all understood that each of us must strive for that: to try to appear to oneself in one's apotheosis. It is into yourself, finally, that for a few minutes the performance changes you. Your brief tomb illuminates us. You are enclosed within it while at the same time your image keeps escaping from it. The wonder is that you have the power to fix yourself there, both in the arena and in heaven, in the form of a constellation. This privilege is reserved for few heroes.

But, for ten seconds—is that a little?—you shine.

During your practice, do not despair at having forgotten your skill. You begin by showing much ability, but shortly you must give up hope for the wire, the somersaults, the Circus, and the dance.

You will know a bitter period—a sort of Hell—and it is after this passage through the dark forest that you will rise again, master of your art.

One of the most moving mysteries is this: after a brilliant period, every artist will cross a desperate land, risking losing his reason and his mastery. If he emerges victorious ...

Your somersaults—do not be afraid of thinking of them as a herd of animals. In you, they lived in a wild state. Uncertain of themselves, they tore each other up, mutilated each other, or mated at random. Pacify your herd of leaps, somersaults, and turns. Each one should live intelligently with the other. Proceed, if you like, to crossbreeding, but with care, not with the randomness of caprice. Now you are shepherd of a flock of beasts that up till now had been disordered and pointless. Thanks to your charms, they are submissive and skillful. Your somersaults, your turns, your leaps were in you, and they knew nothing of that; thanks to your charms, they know that they exist and that they are you, making yourself renowned.

These are pointless, clumsy pieces of advice I give you. No one could follow them. But I wanted nothing else: than to write a poem about this art whose heat would rise to your cheeks. It was a question of inflaming you, not teaching you.

## § 8   Rembrandt's Secret

A strong kindness. And it's to get started quickly that I use this word. His last portrait seems to say something like this: "I will be of such an intelligence that even wild animals will know my kindness." The morality that propels him is not the vain search for finery of the soul; it's his profession that requires it, or rather brings it along with it. It is possible for us to know this, since by a chance almost unique in the history of art, a painter who poses before the mirror with an almost narcissistic complacency is going to leave us, parallel to his body of work, a series of self-portraits in which we will be able to read the evolution of his method and the effect of this evolution on the man. Is that it, or just the opposite?

In the pictures painted before 1642, Rembrandt is seemingly in love with pomp, but a pomp that exists nowhere but in the scene represented. Sumptuousness—as in the portraits of Orientals, biblical scenes—is in the richness of the settings, of the clothes; Jeremiah wears a very pretty robe, he places his foot on a rich rug, on the rock the vases are gold, as we can see. We feel that Rembrandt is happy to invent or represent a conventional richness, as he is happy to paint the extravagant *Saskia as Flora*, or himself with Saskia on his knees, magnificently dressed, raising his glass. Of course, from his youth on, he painted people of humble background—often adorning them with luxurious finery—but it seems that Rembrandt dreamed of pomp, while at the same time his predilection seemed to tend toward the humility of faces. A sensuality—aside from rare exceptions—which flows into his hand when he is going to paint some cloth—for instance—withdraws itself as soon as he touches the face. Even when young, he seemed to prefer faces worked over by ageing.

Through sympathy, perhaps, through a taste for the difficulty (or ease?) of painting, thanks to the problem posed by an ancestor's face? Who knows? But these faces are then accepted in their "picturesque"-ness. He paints them tastefully, skillfully, but—even the one of his mother—without love. Wrinkles are scrupulously noted, crow's feet, the folds of skin, the warts, but they are not prolonged to the inside of the canvas, they are not fed by the heat that comes from a living organism: they are ornaments. It is the two portraits of Mme. Trip (National Gallery) that are painted with the greatest love, those two old-women's heads that are decomposing, rotting before our eyes. I will later on have to say why I use the word "love" when the painter's method becomes so cruel. Here, decrepitude is no longer considered and reconstructed as something picturesque, but as a thing as loveable as anything else. If one were to wash *His Mother Reading*, beneath the wrinkles, one would find the charming young woman she continues to be. We will not wash away the decrepitude of Mme. Trip, she is only that, which appears in all its force. It is there. Bursting forth. Its obviousness is so perceptible it pierces the veil of the picturesque.

Agreeable to the eye or not, decrepitude exists. And thus is beautiful. And rich with. . . . Have you ever had a cut, on the elbow for example, that became infected? There's a scab. With your nails, you remove it. Underneath, filaments of pus that feed this scab continue on for a long way. . . . Good Lord, it's the entire organism that's at work *for* this wound. Each square centimeter of a metacarpal or a lip of Mme. Trip is the same. Who accomplished that? A painter who wanted to render only what is, and who, painting it with exactitude, could represent only all its force—thus its beauty? Or, is he a man who, having understood—by dint of meditation?—that everything has its dignity, he must instead devote himself to representing what seems to lack it?

It has been written that Rembrandt, unlike Hals, for instance, was poor at grasping the likeness of his models; in other words, at seeing the difference between one man and the next. If he didn't see it, perhaps it didn't exist? Or maybe it's all trompe l'oeil? In fact, his portraits rarely reveal to us a character trait of the model: the man who is there is not, a priori, either weak, or cowardly, or tall, or short, or good, or evil: yet he is capable, at any instant, of being such. But we never see a caricatured feature prompted by a first impression. Nor do we see, as in Frans Hals, that sparkling, but fugitive humor: it could be there, but like anything else.

Except for the smiling Titus—that's his son—there's not one face that is serene. They all seem to contain an extremely heavy, thick drama. The individuals, almost always, in their collected, contained attitudes, are like a tornado held for a second at bay. They embody a dense destiny, precisely evaluated by them, and which, any minute now, they will "act on" to the end. Whereas, Rembrandt's drama seems to be only his gaze at the world. He wants to know what's going on so he can free himself of it. His figures, all of them, are aware of the existence of a wound, and they are taking refuge from it. Rembrandt knows he is wounded, but he wants to be cured. From that knowledge comes this impression of vulnerability we get when we look at his self-portraits and the impression of confident strength when we are faced with other paintings.

Without a doubt, this man, well before his maturity, had recognized the dignity of every being and every object, even the humblest, but it was first as if out of a sort of sentimental attachment to its origin. In his drawings, the delicacy with which he treats the most familiar attitudes is not exempt from sentimentality. At the same time, his natural sensuality, along with his imagination, made him wish for luxury and dream of pomp.

His reading of the Bible exalts his imagination: buildings, vases, weapons, furs, rugs, turbans. . . . It is the Old Testament especially that inspires him and his theatricality. He paints. He is famous. He becomes rich. He is proud of his success. Saskia is covered with gold and velvet. . . . She dies. If nothing remains but the world, and painting to approach it, the world has only—or more precisely is only—one single value. And *this* is nothing more than *that*, and nothing less.

But he doesn't rid himself overnight of so many mental habits or so much sensuality. It seems that he will, little by little, try to get rid of them, but not by rejecting them: by transforming them, so they can become useful. He still clings to pomp—I'm speaking of an imaginary, dreamed-of pomp—and to a certain theatricality. To protect himself from them, he will make them undergo a curious treatment: he will at once exalt conventional sumptuousness and at the same time distort it in such a way that it will be impossible to identify it. He will go further. He will cause this brilliance that makes them seem precious to manifest in the most wretched materials, so that everything will be confused. Nothing will be what it seems, but what will secretly illuminate the humblest substance is the not-yet-extinguished fire of an old taste for luxury that, instead of being *on* the canvas and the object represented, will be put *inside*.

This process, brought about slowly and perhaps obscurely, will teach him that each face has value and that it refers—or leads—to one human identity that is equal to another.

As to painting, the twenty-three-year-old miller's son knew how to paint, and admirably too, but at thirty-seven, he has lost the knack. Now he has to learn everything, with an almost clumsy hesitation, without ever venturing virtuosity. And slowly, he will again discover this: each object possesses its own magnificence, neither more nor less than any other; but he, Rembrandt, must reconstruct it, and that brings him to offering us the singular magnificence of color. One could say that he is the only painter in the world respectful of both painting and the model, exalting one as well as the other, one by the other. But what moves us so strongly in his paintings that strive so desperately for the exaltation of everything—without concern for hierarchy—is a sort of reflection, or more precisely, an inner ember, perhaps not nostalgia, but still badly extinguished, and which is what remains of that dreamed-of luxuriousness and of an almost completely used-up theatricality, signs that a life was caught, like any life, in convention, and that it made use of it. And how! Without destroying it, but by transforming it, twisting it, using it, burning it. And it's the signs of an outer ceremony that now come to illuminate, here, anything at all, but from within.

Rembrandt? Except in a few arrogant portraits, everything reveals, from his youth on, an uneasy man in pursuit of a fugitive truth. The acuity of his eye is not wholly explained by the necessity to stare at the mirror. Sometimes he even has a mean look (remember that he'll go so far as to pay to have a creditor thrown into the slammer!), vain (the arrogance of the ostrich feather on the velvet hat . . . and the gold chains . . . ); little by little, the hardness of the face will lessen. Before the mirror, narcissistic complacency has become anxiety and passionate, then trembling search.

For some time now, he has been living with Hendrijke, and this wonderful woman (apart from the portraits of Titus, only those of Hendrijke are full of the sublime old bear's tenderness and gratitude) must satisfy both his sensuality and his need for tenderness. In his last self-portraits, we can no longer read any psychological indication. If we try, we might see something like an air of kindness pass through them. Or detachment? Whatever you like, here it's the same.

Toward the end of his life, Rembrandt became good. Whether it retracts it, breaks it, or masks it, maliciousness makes a screen between the world. Maliciousness, and every form of aggression, and everything we call character traits, our humors, our desires, eroticism, and vanities. Pierce the screen, then, to see the world approach! But Rembrandt did not seek out this goodness—or detachment, if you like—to observe a moral or religious rule (it is in his moments of abandon alone that an artist can have faith, if he ever has it) or to earn a few virtues. When he commits what we call his characteristics to the fire, it is in order to have a purer vision of the world, and with it to make a truer work of art. I think at bottom he didn't care about being good or mean, angry or patient, rapacious or generous. . . . He had to be nothing more than a gaze and a hand. Moreover, by this egoistic path, he had to win—what a word!—that kind of purity, so evident in his last portrait that we are almost hurt by it. But it is by the narrow path of painting that he arrives there.

If I had, schematically, coarsely, to recall that progress—one of the most heroic of modern times—I would say that in 1642—but already the man was not ordinary—unhappiness overtakes and makes desperate an ambitious young man, full of talent, but full also of violence, vulgarity, and exquisite delicacy.

Without hoping ever to see happiness reappear, with a terrible effort, he will try, since only painting remains, to destroy in his work and in himself all the signs of the old vanity, signs, too, of his happiness and his dreams. He wants both to represent the world, since that's the aim of painting, and to make it unrecognizable. Does he realize this right away? This double demand makes him give the painting as material object an importance equal to what it must represent, and then, little by little, this exaltation of painting, since it cannot be conducted abstractly (but the sleeve in *The Jewish Bride* is an abstract painting!), leads him to the exaltation of everything that is to be represented, which nonetheless he wants to make unidentifiable.

This effort brings him to rid himself of all that could lead him back to a differentiated, discontinuous, hierarchic vision of the world: a hand has the same value as a face, a face as the corner of a table, a table corner as a stick, a stick as a hand, a hand as a sleeve . . . and all that, which is perhaps true with other painters—but what painter, up to now, has made something lose its identity in order to exalt it more?—all that, I say, relates back to first the hand, the sleeve, then to painting, of course, but starting from that instant, endlessly from one to the other, and in a dizzying pursuit, toward nothing.

And they have passed through here, too, theatricality, conventional sumptuousness: but burned, consumed, they no longer serve any purpose other than solemnity!

Between 1666 and 1669 there must have been something else in Amsterdam besides the paintings of an old crook (if that story of the repossessed engraving plates is true?) and besides the city. There was what remained of a person reduced to extremes, having almost completely disappeared, going from bed to easel, from easel to toilet—where he must still have sketched with his dirty fingernails—and what remained must have been scarcely anything but a cruel goodness, close to, not far from imbecility. A chapped hand that held brushes dipped in red and brown, an eye resting on objects, nothing but that, but the intelligence that connected the eye to the world was without hope.

With his final portrait, he gently enjoys himself. Quietly. He knows all that a painter can learn. This, first of all (finally, maybe?): that the painter is wholly in the gaze that goes from the object to the canvas, but especially in the gesture of the hand that goes from the little pool of color to the canvas.

The painter is gathered into the calm, certain course of his hand. More than that, into the world: this calm, trembling exchange through which all ceremonies, all luxuries, all fears are transferred. Legally, he has nothing. By juggling with the books, everything is in the hands of Hendrijke the Admirable and Titus. Rembrandt will not even own the canvases he paints.

A man has just passed entirely into his work. What remains of him is enough for the journey, but before, just before, he still has to paint *The Return of the Prodigal Son*.

He dies before having had the temptation to clown around.

# § 9   What Remains of a Rembrandt Torn into Little Squares All the Same Size and Shot Down the Toilet

It's only those kinds of truths, the ones that are not demonstrable and even "*false*," the ones that one cannot without absurdity lead to their conclusion without coming to the negation of them and of oneself—those are the ones that must be exalted by the work of art. They will never have the good—or bad—luck to be applied someday. May they live by the song that they have become and that they revive.

· · · · · · · · · · · · ·

Something that seemed to me like a rottenness was in the process of corrupting my entire former vision of the world. When, one day, in a train compartment, while looking at the passenger sitting opposite me, I had the revelation that every man *is worth as much as* every other, I did not suspect—but that's not true, I knew it obscurely, for suddenly a

*Our gaze can be quick or slow, it depends on the thing observed as much as on us, or more. That is why I speak of that speed which, for instance, precipitates the object in front of us, or of a slowness that weighs it down.*

*When it rests on a painting by Rembrandt (one of those from the end of his life), our gaze becomes heavy, a little bovine. Something holds it, a somber force. Why do we keep looking when we are not at first enchanted by the intellectual rejoicing that knows everything all at once—about a Guardi arabesque, for instance?*

*Like the smell of a cow barn: when I see only the bust or head of people (Hendrijke in*

layer of sadness engulfed me, and, more or less endurable, but always perceptible, it never left me—that this knowledge would bring about such a methodical disintegration. Behind what was visible of this man, or farther—farther away, and at the same time miraculously and distressingly close—inside this man—body and face without grace, ugly, in some details, even vile: dirty moustache, which wouldn't count for much, except it was heavy, stiff, the hairs stuck almost horizontally above the tiny mouth, a spoiled mouth, gobs of spit he aimed between his knees on the floor of the compartment already dirty with cigarette butts, paper, crusts of bread, in short, what in those days made up the dirtiness of a third-class compartment, by the look that stumbled against my own, I discovered, experiencing it as a shock, a sort of universal identity with all men.

No! It didn't happen so quickly, and not in that order: first my gaze stumbled (not crossed, but stumbled . . . ) against the traveler's, or rather was dissolved in that gaze. This man had just raised his eyes from a newspaper and quite simply had placed them, no doubt inadvertently, on my own, which, in the same accidental way, were looking at him. Did he immediately experience

*Berlin), I can't help imagining them standing in manure. Chests breathe. The hands are warm. Bony, knotted, but warm. The table of the Cloth Makers' Guild stands on straw, the five syndics smell of manure and cow shit. Under Hendrijke's skirts, under the fur-lined cloaks, under the frock coats, under the painter's extravagant robe, the bodies dutifully carry out their functions: they digest, they are hot, they are heavy, they smell, they shit.— As delicate as her face is and as serious her gaze, The Jewish Bride has an ass. We can tell. Any instant now she can raise her skirts. She can sit down, she's got plenty. Mme. Trip, too. As for Rembrandt himself, let's not speak of him: from his first portrait on, his fleshly mass will continue to accelerate from one painting to another until the last one, where he arrives, definitive, but not emptied of substance. After he had lost what was dearest to him—his mother and wife— you could say that this tough guy sought to lose himself, abandoning civility toward the people of Amsterdam, and disappeared socially.*

the same emotion—and immediate disarray—as I did? His gaze was not that of another person: it was my own I met in a mirror, *by accident and in solitude and forgetting myself.* What I experienced I could convey only in this form: I flowed out of my body, through my eyes, into the traveler's, *at the same time that the traveler flowed into my own.* Or rather: *I had flowed,* for the look was so brief that I can recall it only with the help of this tense of the verb. The traveler returned to his reading. Stupefied by what I had just discovered, only then did I think of examining the unknown man, and I came away with the impression of disgust described earlier: beneath his crumpled, rough, dingy clothes, his body must have been dirty and wrinkled. His mouth was soft and protected by a badly trimmed moustache, I told myself that this man was probably spineless, maybe cowardly. He was over fifty. The train continued its indifferent course through French villages. Night was falling. The idea of passing the twilight minutes, those of complicity, with this companion greatly disturbed me.

What was it, then, that had flowed out of my body—I fl . . . —and what part of the traveler flowed out of his body?

*To want to be nothing is a phrase one often hears. It is Christian: Must we understand that man seeks to lose, to let dissolve, what in some way banally singularizes him, what gives him his opacity, so that on the day of his death, he can present himself to God as pure transparency, not even iridescent? I don't know, and I don't care.*

*For Rembrandt, his entire work makes me think that it wasn't enough for him to get rid of what encumbered him to bring about this transparency described above, but to transform it, to change it, to make it serve the work of art. To rid the subject of whatever anecdotal quality it has and position it under a light of eternity. Recognized by today, by tomorrow, but also by the dead. A work offered to the living of today and tomorrow, but not to the dead of all ages, what use would that be?*

*A painting by Rembrandt not only stops time, which was making the subject flow into the future, but makes it go back to the earliest eras. By this process, Rembrandt invokes solemnity. And he*

This disagreeable experience did not happen again, either in its fresh suddenness or in its intensity, but its consequences within me have never stopped being felt. What I experienced on the train seemed to me like a revelation: after the accidents—in this case repugnant—of his appearance, this man contained, and let me detect, what made him identical to me. (I wrote that sentence first, but I corrected it with this, more precise and more distressing: I knew I was identical to this man.)

Was that because every man is identical to every other?

Continuing to meditate during the journey, and in a sort of disgust with myself, I quickly came to believe that it was this sameness that allowed every man to be loved, *neither more nor less* than any other, and that allowed even the most revolting appearance to be loved, that is to say, taken charge of and recognized, cherished. That wasn't all. My meditations were to lead me to this: this appearance, which I had first called vile, was—the word is not too strong—*required* by this sameness [*identité*] (this word kept coming back, but maybe because I did not yet have at my disposal a very rich vocabulary) which kept circulating among all men, and of which a single glance, in its abandon, became

*discovers why each instant, each event, is solemn: for that, his own solitude teaches him.*

*But one must also restore this solemnity to the canvas, and that is when his taste for theatricality—so keen when he was twenty-five—will be useful to him. It is possible that his immense grief—Saskia's death—turned Rembrandt away from all the pleasures of every day, and that he filled his mourning by changing gold chains, feathered hats, swords, into values, or rather, into pictorial celebrations. I don't know if he cried, this beefy Dutchman, but around '42 he knew the baptism of fire, and little by little, his first, vain, bold nature is going to be transformed.*

*For at the age of twenty, the strapping fellow doesn't look very easygoing, and he spends his time in front of the mirror. He loves himself, he falls for himself, so young and already in the mirror! Not to fix himself up and run to the ball, but to look at himself for a long time, with complacency, alone: Rembrandt, with the three moustaches, with the frowning eyebrows,* aware. I even thought I understood that this appearance was the temporary form of the identity of all men. But that pure, almost insipid look that circulated from one traveler to the other, in which their will could do nothing, which their will might perhaps have prevented, lasted just an instant, and that was enough for a profound sadness to cast its shadow on me and make its home in me. I lived for quite a while with this discovery, which I deliberately kept secret, and the memories of which I tried to distance from me, but still, some part in me watched over a stain of sadness that, suddenly, as if filled by a breath, darkened everything.

"Every man," I said to myself, the revelation had come to me, "behind his charming or to our eyes monstrous appearance, retains a quality that seems to be like a last resort and that makes him, in a most secret, perhaps irreducible domain, what every man is."

Did I even think I found this equivalence at Les Halles, at the slaughterhouses, in the fixed, but not sightless eyes of the sheep's heads, cut, piled in pyramids on the sidewalk? Where should I stop? Who would I have murdered if I had killed some cheetah walking with long strides, supple as a villain from long ago?

*with the disheveled hair, the wild eyes, etc. No anxiety is visible in this simulated quest for self. If he paints buildings, they are always operatic scenery. Then, little by little, without distancing himself from his narcissism or from his taste for theatricality, he will change them: the former in order to arrive at anxiety, to the confusion he will overcome, the latter to extract the joys—also wild—from the sleeve of* The Jewish Bride.

*As soon as Saskia dies—I wonder if he didn't kill her, one way or another, if he didn't rejoice at her death— finally his eye and hand are free. From this moment on, he undertakes a sort of debauchery in painting: with Saskia dead, the world and the opinions of society have little weight. We must imagine it, Saskia dying and him in his studio, perched on ladders, breaking up the arrangement of the* Nightwatch. *Does he believe in God? Not when he paints. He knows the Bible, and he uses it.*

*It goes without saying that everything I've just said hasn't the least importance unless you accept that the*

You will remember that earlier I had said that my dearest friends took refuge, I was certain, entirely in a secret wound. But not long after, I wrote "in a most secret, perhaps irreducible domain." Was I speaking of the same thing? One man was identical to another, that's what hit me. But was it, then, so rare to learn that, which amazes me, and how could it further me to know it? First, it's a different thing to know something wholly in an analytical way than to grasp it by a sudden intuition. (For I had of course heard it said around me, and I had read, that all men are equal, and even that they are brothers.) But how could this further me? One thing was more certain: I could no longer not know what I had known in the train.

How—I was incapable of seeing—how did I pass from this knowledge that every man is like every other to the idea that every man is all other men? But the idea was now inside me. It was there like a certainty. More precisely—but I'm going to spoil it—it could have been expressed by this aphorism: "In the world there exists and there has never existed anything but one single man. He is entirely in each of us, thus he is ourselves. Each one is the other and the others. In the abandon of night, a clear, exchanged look—

*whole of it is more or less false. The work of art, if it is complete, does not permit conclusions, intellectual games, to be drawn from it. It even seems to confuse the intelligence, or to tie it in knots. Now I've played that game, too.*

*In a way, works of art would make us idiots, if their fascination weren't the proof— uncontrollable, but unarguable—that this paralysis of the intelligence is mixed with the most luminous certainty. Which certainty, I have no idea. At the origin of these lines there is my emotion (in London twelve years ago) in front of his most beautiful paintings.—What do I have, then? What are these paintings that I find so hard to get out of my mind? Who is this Mrs. Trip? This Mister ...*

*No. I never asked myself who these ladies or gentlemen were. And maybe it's this more or less clear-cut absence of question that makes me wince? The more I looked at them, the less these portraits reminded me of anyone. Of no one. No doubt I needed a long time to arrive at this hopeless and intoxicating* drawn-out or fleeting, I ignored technical details—made us aware of it. Except that a phenomenon, for which I don't even know a name, seems infinitely to divide this single man, splits him into the accidents of appearance, and makes each of the fragments foreign to us."

I explained myself clumsily, and what I experienced was even stronger and more confused than this idea of which I spoke, which, rather than a thought, was dreamed, engendered, dragged, or dredged up by a somewhat listless daydreaming.

No man was my brother: each man was myself, but isolated, temporarily, in his particular shell. But this observation did not lead me to examine all morals or see them in a new light. Toward this me outside of my particular appearance I experienced no tenderness, no affection. Nor toward the form taken by the other—or his prison. Or his tomb? Instead, I seemed to be as pitiless with it as I had been with this shape that answered to my name and that was writing these lines. The sadness that had swooped down upon me is what troubled me most. After the moment I had this revelation while gazing at the unknown passenger, it was impossible for me to see the world as I used to. Nothing was certain. The world suddenly floated. I

*idea: the portraits made by Rembrandt (after his fifties) refer to no identifiable person. No detail, no physiognomic trait refers to a particular characteristic or psychology. Are they depersonalized by oversimplification? Not at all. Think of Margaretha Trip's wrinkles. And the more I looked at them, hoping to grasp, or approach, the personality, as they say, to discover their particular identity, the more they escaped—all of them—in an infinite flight, and at the same speed. Only Rembrandt himself—maybe because of the acuity of his gaze scrutinizing his own image—kept a little particularity: or at least attention. But the others, if I had deemed negligible this profound sadness, fled without allowing anything of them to be grasped.*

*Negligible, this sadness? The sadness of being in the world? Nothing other than the attitude assumed naturally by beings when they are alone, waiting to act, like this or like that. Rembrandt himself, in his portrait in Cologne, where he is laughing. The face and background are so* remained for a long time as if sickened by my discovery, but I felt that it wouldn't be long before this was going to force me into serious changes, which would be renunciations. My sadness was an indication. The world was changed. In a third-class carriage, between Salon and Saint-Rambert-d'Albon, it had just lost its beautiful colors, its charm. Already I was nostalgically saying goodbye to them, and it wasn't without sadness or disgust that I embarked on those paths that would be ever more solitary, especially in those visions of the world that, instead of exalting my joy, caused me so much dismay.

"Soon," I told myself, "nothing of what used to be so precious will count: love affairs, friendships, forms, vanity, everything that has to do with seduction."

But was this gaze that rested on the passenger and that was so atrociously revealing possible perhaps because of an ancient disposition of the mind, because of my life, or any other reason? I wasn't very sure that another man could have felt himself flow out, through his gaze, into another's body, or that the significance of this sensation for him would have been the one I offered here. Still tempted to call into question the plenum of the world, was I

*red that the whole painting makes one think of a placenta dried in the sun.*

*You don't have much room to stand back, in the museum in Cologne. You have to position yourself diagonally, at an angle. It's from there I looked at him, but the head— mine—lowered, turned sort of upside down. The blood came to my head, but how sad this laughing face was!*

*It's beginning with the time that he depersonalizes his models and that he removes all identifiable characteristics from objects that he gives the most weight, the greatest reality, to both.*

*Something important has happened: at the same time as he recognizes the object, his eye recognizes the painting, as such. And it will never leave it. Rembrandt no longer distorts the painting by trying to confuse it with the object or face it is charged with representing: he presents it as distinct substance, not ashamed of being what it is. Openness of fields ploughed in the morning, smoking. What the spectator gains, I don't yet know, but the painter gains* here again trying to pour myself into individual shells in order better to deny singularity?

"Soon, nothing more will count. . . ." Or nothing would be changed? If each enclosure, preciously, contains one single identity, each enclosure is unique and succeeds in establishing between each of us an opposition that seems irremediable, in creating an innumerable variety of individuals who think of themselves as: self-other. Might each man have nothing precious or real except this singularity: "his" moustache, "his" eyes, "his" clubfoot, "his" harelip? And if he had nothing to take pride in but the size of "his" cock? But this gaze went from the unknown passenger to me, and the immediate certainty that self-other were only one, at the same time both me-or-him, and me-and-him? How can I forget that mucus?

Let's go on. Knowing what I had just learned, I didn't have to direct my efforts according to the indications of the revelation in order to dissolve myself into an approximate contemplation. I simply could not avoid knowing what I knew, and no matter what the cost, I had to pursue its consequences, whatever they were. Since various incidents in my life had forced me into poetry, perhaps the poet had to use this new

*full title to his profession. He presents himself in his madness of daubing, mad with color, losing the airs and hypocrisy of pretenders. This will be perceptible in the final paintings. But Rembrandt had to recognize and accept himself as a being of flesh—what am I saying, of flesh?—of meat, raw meat, of blood, of tears, of sweat, of shit, of intelligence and tenderness, of other things, too, ad infinitum, but with none of them negating the others, or better: each one hailing the others.*

*And it goes without saying that Rembrandt's entire oeuvre has no meaning—at least for me—unless I know that what I have just written is false.*

discovery for himself. But above all,
I had to notice this: the only
moments of my life that I could
think of as true, ripping open my
appearance and revealing . . . what?
*a solid void* that kept perpetuating
me?—I knew during some truly holy
rages, in some equally blessed
moments of fear, and in the ray of
light—the first—that went from a
young man's eye to my own, in our
exchanged look. Finally in this gaze
passing from the passenger into me.
The rest, all the rest, seemed to me
the effect of an optical error provoked by my appearance, itself necessarily deceptive. Rembrandt was
the first to accuse me. Rembrandt!
That severe finger that spreads open
the rags and shows . . . what? An
infinite, an infernal transparency.

So I experienced a profound disgust for what I had been heading
toward, which I didn't know, and
which, thank God, I couldn't avoid,
and then a great sadness for what I
was going to lose of myself. Everything became disillusioned around
me, everything rotted. Eroticism and
its furies seemed denied to me, utterly. How to ignore, after the experience on the train, that every attrac-
tive form, if it encloses me, is myself?
But if I tried to grasp this identity,
every form, monstrous or lovable,
lost its power over me.

"The search for the erotic," I told
myself, "is possible only when one
supposes that each being has its individuality, that it is irreducible, and
that physical form is aware of it and
is aware only of it."

What did I know of erotic signifi-
cation? But the idea that I was circulating in each man, that each
man was myself, disgusted me. For a
little while longer, if every somewhat handsome—with conventional
beauty—and male human form still
kept a little power over me, it was,
you could say, by reverberation. This
power was the reflection of the one
to which I had yielded for so long.
Nostalgic goodbye to it, too. Thus,
each person no longer appeared to
me in his total, absolute, magnificent
individuality: as a fragmentary
appearance of one single being, it
made me even sicker. Yet I wrote the
preceding without ceasing to be
unsettled, worked on by the erotic
themes that had been familiar to me
and that had dominated my life. I
was sincere when I spoke of a search
starting from the revelation "that
every man is every other man and I
am like all the others"—but I know
that I was also writing that in order
to rid myself of eroticism, to try to
dislodge it from me, or at least to
distance it. An erect phallus, congested and vibrating, standing in a

thicket of curly black hairs, and after
that: thick thighs, then the torso, the
whole body, the hands, the thumbs,
then the neck, the lips, the teeth, the
nose, the hair, finally the eyes that
summon amorous furies as if for a
rescue or an annihilation, and all
that struggling against this so fragile
look capable perhaps of destroying
this All-Power?

# § 10   That Strange Word ...

That strange word "urbanism," whether it comes from a Pope Urban or from the City, will maybe no longer be concerned with the dead. The living will get rid of their corpses, slyly or not, as one rids oneself of a shameful thought. By hurrying them to the crematorium furnace, the urbanized world will rid itself of a great theatrical aid, and perhaps of theater itself. In place of the cemetery, center—albeit sometimes outlying center—of the city, you'll have columbaria, with chimney, without chimney, with or without smoke, and the dead, charred like scorched rolls of bread, will serve as fertilizer for the kolkhoz or kibbutz, far from the city. Still, if cremation takes on a dramatic allure—either because one single man was solemnly burned and cooked alive or because the Town or State wanted to rid themselves, en masse, so to speak, of another community—the crematorium, like that of Dachau, evocative of a very possible future architecturally escaping time, future as well as past, chimney still maintained by cleaning teams who sing lieder around this slanting, erect phallus of red brick or who just whistle Mozart tunes, and who still maintain the open gullet of this oven where on grates up to ten or twelve corpses at once can be put in the oven—a certain form of theater could be perpetuated, but if the crematoria in cities are made to disappear or are reduced to the dimensions of a grocery store, the theater will die. Of future urban planners we will demand that a cemetery be installed in the town, where the dead will continue to be buried, or to plan a disturbing columbarium, with simple but imperious lines, and then, next to it, in its shadow, or in the midst of the tombs, the theater will be erected. Do you see where I'm heading? The theater will be placed as close as possible, in the truly tutelary shade of the place where the dead are kept, or in the shadow of the only monument that digests them.

I give you these pieces of advice without too much solemnity; I'm dreaming, rather, with the active nonchalance of a child who knows the importance of the theater.

⁓

Among other aims, the theater has that of letting us escape time, which we call historical, but which is theological. From the beginning of the theatrical event, the time that unfolds does not belong to any identifiable calendar. It eludes the Christian era as well as the Revolutionary era. Even if time, which we call historical—I mean the time that unfolds starting from a mythical and controversial event also called the Advent—does not completely disappear from the consciousness of the spectators, another time, which each spectator lives fully, unfolds too, and having neither beginning nor end, it overturns the historical conventions necessitated by social life; suddenly, it also overturns social conventions, and not just for any random chaos, but for that of liberation—the dramatic event being suspended, outside of historically counted time, in its own dramatic time—it is for a breathtaking liberation.

The Christian West, by dint of ruses, does what it can to glue together all the peoples of the world in an era that has its origin in the hypothetical Incarnation. This is nothing other than the "calendar trick," which the West tries to pull over the entire world.

Caught in a named, counted time, starting from an event that is of interest only to the West, the world is at great risk, if it accepts this time, of accepting a rhythm aligned with celebrations in which the entire world will be trapped.

It would seem urgent, then, to multiply the "Advents" starting from which calendars can be established, without any relationship to those that are imperialistically imposed. I even think that any event, private or public, should give birth to a multitude of calendars, in such a way as to put the Christian era and what follows that counted time, starting from the Very Questionable Nativity, out of business.

The theater ...

THE THEATER?

THE THEATER.

~

Where should we go? Toward what form? The place of the theater, containing the stage and the auditorium?

The place. To an Italian who wanted to build a theater with functional components that would be mobile and its architecture changing according to the play being performed, I responded even before he had finished his sentence that the architecture of the theater is yet to be discovered, but it must be fixed, immobilized, so that it can be recognized as responsible: it will be judged on its form. It is too easy to trust what changes. Let us resort, if you like, to the ephemeral, but after the irreversible act for which we will be judged, or, again if you like, the fixed act that judges itself.

~

Since I do not have—if they exist—spiritual powers, I do not demand that the place for the theater be chosen, after an effort of meditation, by a man or by a community capable of this effort, but it is certainly necessary for the architect to discover the sense of theater in the world, and, having understood it, elaborate his work with an almost priestly and smiling gravity. If need be, he should be supported, protected, during his enterprise, by a group of men ignorant of architecture, but capable of true daring in the struggle of meditation, that is to say, of inner laughter.

~

If we—provisionally—accept the common ideas of time and history, admitting, too, that the act of painting did not stay the same as it had been before the invention of photography, it seems that the theater will not remain, after cinema and television, what it was before them. As long as we have known the theater, it seems that along with its essential function, each play was full of preoccupations about politics, religion, morality, or anything, transforming the dramatic action into a didactic means.

Maybe—I will still say "maybe," since I am a man, and alone— maybe television and cinema will better fulfill an educative function: while the theater will find itself emptied, perhaps purged, of what encumbered it, maybe it will be able to shine from its sole virtue(s)—which is, or are, perhaps still to be discovered.

⁓

Aside from a few paintings—or fragments in paintings—the painters before the discovery of photography who left us testimony of a vision and a painter freed from all concern for stupidly obvious resemblances are rare. Not daring to deal too much— except Frans Hals (*The Women Regents* [*of the Haarlem Almshouse*])—with the face, the painters who dared to serve both the object painted and painting itself took a flower or a dress as pretext (Velasquez, Rembrandt, Goya). It is possible that, faced with the results of photography, painters remained sheepish. After they rallied, they discovered what painting still was.

In the same way, or in a similar way, playwrights remained sheepish faced with what television and the cinema allow. If they accept the fact—if it is a fact—that the theater cannot compete with such excessive methods—those of TV and cinema—writers for the theater will discover the virtues unique to the theater, which, perhaps, have to do only with myth.

⁓

Politics, history, classic psychological demonstrations, evening entertainment itself will have to give way to something more, I don't know how to say it, but maybe more sparkling. All that shit, all that manure will be eliminated.— You'll understand that the slightly controversial words are not shit or manure. I will remark, moreover, that these words and the situations they summon are so numerous in my theater because they have been "forgotten" in most plays: words and situations regarded as coarse have crowded into and taken refuge in my work, my plays, where they have received the right of asylum. If my theater stinks, it's because the other kind smells nice.

～

Drama, that is to say, the theatrical act at the instant of its presentation, this theatrical act cannot be just anything, but inside anything it can find its pretext. It seems to me in fact that any event, visible or not, if it is isolated, I mean fragmented in the continuum, can, if it is well directed, serve as pretext or even be the point of departure and arrival for the theatrical act. That is, any event lived by us, in one way or another, but whose burning we have felt, caused by a fire that can be extinguished only if it is stirred up. Politics, entertainments, morality, etc., have nothing to do with our intentions. If, despite ourselves, they slip into the theatrical act, they should be chased out until all traces are erased: they are the dross that can be used to make movies, TV, cartoons, *romans-photo*—ah, there's a whole graveyard of those junked cars.

～

But drama itself? With the author, it has its dazzling beginning, so it is up to him to capture this lightning and organize, starting from the illumination that shows the void, a verbal architecture—that's to say grammatical and ceremonial—cunningly showing that from this void an appearance that shows the void rips itself free.

～

We should note in passing that the attitude of Christian prayer, with eyes and head lowered, does not favor meditation. It's a physical attitude that summons a closed, submissive intellectual attitude, it discourages a spiritual attempt. If you choose this position, God could come, swoop down on your neck, place his mark, and it could last for a long time. To meditate, one has to discover an open attitude—not of challenge—but not of abandonment to God. You have to watch out. A little too much submission and God ships you a blessing: you've had it.

～

In today's cities, the only place—unfortunately, only near the outskirts—where a theater could be built is the cemetery. The choice will benefit both the cemetery and the theater. The architect of the theater will not be able to tolerate the inane constructions where families enclose their dead.

Demolish the mausoleums. Maybe preserve a few ruins: a piece of a column, a pediment, an angel's wing, a broken urn, to indicate that a vengeful indignation demanded this preliminary drama so that the vegetation, and maybe some sturdy weeds, born in the mass of rotting bodies, can level out the field of the dead. If a site is reserved for the theater, the audience (when arriving and departing) will have to walk on paths that run alongside the tombs. Think of the spectators' exit after Mozart's *Don Giovanni*, leaving amid the dead lying underground, before returning to secular life. Neither the conversations nor the silence would be the same as at the exit of a Parisian theater.

Death should be at once closer and lighter, the theater more serious.

There are other reasons. They are more subtle. It is up to you to discover them within you without defining them or naming them.

～

Monumental theater—whose style is yet to be discovered—must have as much importance as the Palace of Justice, as the monuments to the dead, as the cathedral, as the Chamber of Deputies, as the War College, as government headquarters, as the clandestine venues of the black market or for drugs, as the Observatory—and its function must be all those at once, but in a certain way: in a cemetery, or quite close to the crematorium furnace, to the stiff, tilting, phallic chimney.

～

I'm not speaking of a dead cemetery, but a live one, not the kind where only a few gravestones remain. I'm speaking of a cemetery where graves would continue to be dug and the dead buried, I'm speaking of a Crematorium where corpses are cooked day and night.

～

Page 4[1] will show you how, schematically and clumsily, I see the placement of a new theater. When I speak there of a privileged audience, it is a question of certain people who will be adequately educated to comment on theater in general and on the play performed that day.

∽

Without becoming too preoccupied with the theater, it seems to me that the important thing is not to multiply the number of performances so that a large number of spectators can profit from them (?) but to arrange it so that the trials—which they call rehearsals—end up in one single performance, whose intensity and brilliance would be so great that, by what it will have set ablaze in each spectator, it would be enough to illuminate those who weren't able to be present and stir up trouble in them.

∽

As to the audience, only those would come who knew they were capable of a nighttime walk in a cemetery to be confronted with a mystery.

If such a location were used, as much a part of urbanism as of culture, writers would be less frivolous, they'd think twice before having plays performed there. They might accept the omens of insanity, or of a frivolity bordering on insanity.

∽

With a sort of easy grace, cemeteries, after a certain amount of time, allow themselves to be dispossessed. When the dead are no longer buried there, they die, but in an elegant way: lichens, saltpeter, moss cover the slabs. The theater built in the cemetery might die—it will go out—like it. Might it disappear? It is possible that the art of the theater may someday disappear. We must accept the notion. If one day the activity of men were revolutionary day after day, the theater would have lost its place in life. If dullness of mind one day evoked only daydreams in men, the theater would also die.

∽

To look for the origins of the theater in History, and the origin of History in time, is idiotic. A waste of time.

What would we lose if we lost the theater?

∽

What will the cemeteries be? An oven capable of disintegrating the dead. If I speak of a theater among the tombs, it's because the word "death" today is shadowy, and in a world that seems to be going so cheerfully toward the luminosity of analysis, our transparent eyelids no longer protected, like Mallarmé, I think a little darkness must be added. Science deciphers everything, or wants to, but we've had it! We must take refuge, and nowhere else but in our ingeniously lit entrails. . . . No, I'm wrong: not take refuge, but discover a fresh and scorching shadow, which will be our work.

∼

Even if the graves have grown indistinct, the cemetery will be well kept up, the Crematorium too. During the day, joyful teams—Germany has a few—will clean them, whistling, but just whistling. The inside of the oven and of the chimney can remain black with soot.

∼

Where? Rome, did I read this, had—but perhaps my memory deceives me—a funeral mime. His role? Preceding the procession, he was supposed to mime the most important deeds that made up the life of the dead man when he—the dead man—was alive.

Improvise gestures, attitudes?

Words. Living, I don't know how, the French language hides and reveals a war that words make, enemy brothers, one tearing itself away from the other or becoming infatuated with it. If tradition and treason were born from one single original gesture and diverge so each can live its individual life, how is it that they are linked in their distortion all through language?

Living no more poorly than any other, yet this language, like others, allows words to overlap each other like animals in heat, and what comes out of our mouth is an orgy of words that mate, innocently or not, and that give French discourse the salubrious air of a forested country where all the wandering animals begin. Writing in such a language—or speaking it—one says nothing. One just allows a torrent of beings, or, if you like, of ambiguous words, like the beasts of the Fable, to mill about some more, to mingle and mix, in the midst of vegetation that is itself distracted, patterned by its mixtures of pollen, by its random grafts, by its sprouts, its cuttings.

If anyone expects that by means of such a proliferation—or luxuriance—of monsters he can handle a coherent discourse, he is mistaken: at best he breeds larval and sly swarms similar to the processions of processionary caterpillars, which exchange their sperm to give birth to a grotesque progeny without any progress, without importance, come hither from Greek, Saxon, Levantine, Bedouin, Latin, Gaelic, from a wandering Chinese, from three Mongolian vagabonds, and which speak not to say anything, but, by mating, to reveal a verbal orgy whose meaning is lost, not in the night of time, but in the infinity of tender or brutal mutations.

And the funeral mime?

And the Theater in the cemetery?

Before burying the dead man, the corpse in its coffin should be borne just in front of the stage; friends, enemies, and onlookers should be up in the part reserved for the public; the funeral mime preceding the procession should split in two and multiply; he should become a troupe of actors, and, in front of the dead man and the audience, he should make the dead man live and die again; then the coffin should be lifted and carried, in the middle of the night, to the grave; finally the audience should depart: the celebration is over. Until a new ceremony offered by another dead man whose life will deserve a dramatic, not tragic performance. One must live tragedy, not play it.

When one is clever, one can pretend to understand, one can pretend to think that words do not change, that their meaning is fixed, or that it changes thanks to our intentions, one tries to believe, so if their appearance alters a little, we become gods. Whereas I, facing this enraged herd caged in the dictionary, I know that I have said nothing and that I will never say anything: and the words couldn't care less.

Deeds are scarcely more docile. As in the case of language, there is a grammar of action, and beware of the autodidact!

To betray is perhaps traditional, but treason is no repose. I had to make a great effort to betray my friends: in the end, there was a reward.

So, for the great parade before the burial of the corpse, if the funeral mime wants to make the dead man live and die again, he will have to discover, and dare to say them, those dialectophage words that in front of the audience will devour the life and death of the dead man.

# § 11   Interview with Hubert Fichte

HUBERT FICHTE: Yesterday[1] you mentioned a demonstration you were going to.

JEAN GENET: No, I wasn't going; there were demonstrations yesterday that brought together members of the CGT, the CFDT, and the CGC. [CGT: Confédération Générale du Travail (the General Confederation of Labor); CFDT: Confédération française démocratique du travail (French Democratic Confederation of Labor); CGC: Confédération générale des cadres (General confederation of management)—*Trans.*] and the three opposition parties, the Communist Party, the Socialist Party, and the Left Radicals.[2] The official purpose of the demonstration was to protest the economic policies of the government. But in reality, the protest was sparked by the arrest of several union activists and even a few soldiers who were accused of undermining army morale and are in danger of being brought before the state security court, where the sentences can be anywhere from five to twenty years in prison.

HF: So it was a demonstration against Giscard d'Estaing?

JG: It was directed especially against the minister of defense and the minister of the interior.

HF: You're not a member of any of the parties that gathered there?

JG: No, absolutely not. I don't belong to any party!

HF: People say: Jean Genet has no address, he lives in little hotels ...

JG: By chance I happen to have my passport on me. Here's my address, you can read it right there.

HF: It's the address at Gallimard: 5 rue Sébastien-Bottin.

JG: I don't have any other; see, that's my official address.

HF: Does living without an address, without an apartment, make it difficult to maintain friendships? You can't invite anyone over, you can't cook ...

JG: I don't like to cook.

HF: You're always the one who's invited.

JG: So what? Obviously it creates some problems, and therefore some solutions; at the same time, it allows for a certain irresponsibility. I have no social responsibilities, and this allows me a sort of immediate engagement, I can join up on the spot. When Bobby Seale was arrested—he was the head of the Black Panthers—two of the Panthers[3] came to see me and asked me what I could do for Bobby Seale. It was morning, I answered, "The simplest thing would be to go to the United States to see the situation." They said, "When?"—"How about tomorrow?"—"So soon?" I saw that the Panthers were thrown off by this. They were used to moving quickly, but I was moving more quickly than they were, all because I was living in a hotel. I had one small suitcase. If I had an apartment, would I have been able to do that? If I had friendships, would I be able to move around with the same speed?

HF: Are you worried about being surrounded by a certain bourgeois luxury, because of your fame and your resources?

JG: Ah! That's obviously really stupid. No, I don't think so, because I have no respect for bourgeois luxury. I'd need to have a Renaissance castle at least. My royalties aren't enough to buy a court like Borgia's, so I'm not much in danger of that.

HF: What fascinates you about Borgia's court?

JG: I'm not fascinated, I just think that the last manifestations of architectural luxury date from the Renaissance. I don't see much after that. The eighteenth century in France doesn't really do it for me. The same goes for the seventeenth century. The first time I went to the palace of Versailles, I was horrified. The little stone castle is quite lovely, but when you go into the garden and turn around to look at the large façade, it's horrific! I wonder why that guy—who was the architect? Mansart,[4] wasn't it?—in any case, I wonder why Louis XIV didn't multiply the miles of columns? It's heavy, bulky, stupid, and endless. There are palaces in Italy, from the Renaissance, that appear to be very small, but are actually immense, very beautiful and still inhabitable. The Hall of Mirrors, I don't know exactly what the proportions are, but there are better—Brasilia for example.

HF: Doesn't Brasilia seem to you endless and repeatable ad infinitum?

JG: No, I don't think so; there are several distinct parts that come together into a whole, it's very harmonious. I flew over the city. I saw it in the sun, in the rain, at night, in the daytime, and in the wind, the cold, and the heat, and I know Brasilia from the tenth floor of the Hotel Nacional, and also from the street. And yet it's odd that that guy, who's a communist, I mean Oscar Niemeyer,[5] when he created this city, he was unable to prevent shantytowns full of Indians from springing up nearly all the way around it. It would seem that the only people who can live in the huge buildings of Brasilia are six-foot-four hulks with blond or brown hair, well built, in any case, more like statuary than human beings. But in reality, they're inhabited by little functionaries, ambassadors, ministers, and not by the Indians or the Blacks of Brasilia. Still, I can't think of any other city that, like Brasilia, was planned and created from the ground up and that is apparently harmonious. There were some things Oscar Niemeyer didn't understand, he didn't succeed because he didn't have the vision of an urban planner capable of conceiving that he could, that he had to build human housing for a proletariat and that he had to elim-inate everything that would allow class differences to arise. His city pushes out the proletariat and forces it to collect around the periphery. What struck me most was the Palace of Foreign Affairs. The cathedral, the "concrete flower," says nothing at all to me. I went to Matisse's little church in Vence,[6] the one dedicated to a figure I normally can't stand, Saint Dominic. You have to go inside. There is an incredible use of space; you're inside a poem.

HF: There's a similar poetic quality in Romanesque architecture.

JG: Yes.

HF: In Montmajour, or Solignac. Do you know the domed church in Solignac?

JG: Romanesque churches always have domes.

HF: Some have barrel vaults, etc.

JG: They almost always have domes, because the Romanesque arch requires a dome.

HF: By comparing Niemeyer's architecture with Matisse's little chapel, would you say that Matisse is a revolutionary artist?

JG: No. One must be very careful in using the word "revolutionary." Above all it must be used advisedly. It's a difficult word. I wonder if the concept *revolutionary* can be separated from the concept of violence. We have to use other words, other terms, to name what was accomplished, say, by Cézanne. I think that artists like Cézanne and the painters who followed him, or the musicians who challenged the notion of tonality, I think that they were very daring, but not really that much; not that much because on the one hand the absolute dominance of the notions of perspective in painting or the chromatic scale in music was already being eroded, but through wit and irony, through jokes. Alban Berg wrote music without taking himself too seriously, and then later it was more fully elaborated, so in that sense it was audacious, it had a considerable impact, but I think that for them, as an intellectual adventure it didn't have the importance we attribute to them. This might explain why Cézanne remained a very simple man. He went to Mass, he lived with a woman he wasn't married to. The fact that Zola, a childhood friend, didn't understand him, that must have hurt him, but I'm not sure that Cézanne believed he would have a posterity or such posthumous glory.

HF: Yesterday you spoke of Monteverdi. Is this for you an art that brutally breaks with tradition?

JG: For me there is nothing more cheerful, more joyous, than the *Beata Virgine Mass.*

HF: You claim to be a-religious, to be an atheist; how do you approach a work like the *Vespro della beata Virgine*?

JG: Twenty years ago I read the *Iliad* and found it very, very beautiful; do you think I believe in the religion of Zeus?

HF: I think that at bottom you're not far from it, to tell the truth.

JG: When I was in Japan the last time, seven or eight years ago,[7] I saw a Noh play that I found very moving. You know that women's roles are played by men. At a certain moment, an actor was wearing the mask of an old woman, the last Buddhist woman. She goes into a cave, covers herself with a fan, and then uncovers her face, and it's the face of a young girl, the first Shinto woman. The theme was the passage from the Buddhist religion to the Shinto religion. Do you think I'm Buddhist or Shinto?

HF: I think that your work, your whole life, expresses a fascination with ritual.

JG: There's no ritual in the *Iliad*.

HF: In the *Iliad* there is a ritual of description, there are refrains and topoi, for example: "and all his guts poured out on the ground." [*Iliad*, 3.525; Richard Lattimore translation (University of Chicago Press, 1951)—*Trans.*]

JG: No, that's just a manner of speaking, I wonder if those are really Homeric inventions, or if it's not simply a way to move more quickly.

HF: With Homer, the mode of composition is itself almost religious.

JG: In the *Iliad*, yes, but not in the *Odyssey*.

HF: Why do you like Strindberg's *Miss Julie*, and why don't you like the Brecht of *Galileo Galilei*?

JG: Because what Brecht says is nothing but garbage; because *Galileo Galilei* cites the obvious; it tells me things I would have discovered without Brecht. Strindberg, or in any case *Miss Julie*, does not present the obvious. It's very new. I wasn't expecting it. I saw *Miss Julie* after *The Dance of Death*, how do you say it in Swedish?

HF: *Dödsdansen*.

JG: I liked it very much. Nothing Strindberg says could be said in any other way than poetically, and everything Brecht says can be said and in fact has been said prosaically.

HF: That was his intention. He called his theater "epic theater," and he introduced or claimed to introduce the distancing that Strindberg indeed had already achieved in his introduction to *Miss Julie*. Strindberg already assumes a cold spectator, the Brechtian spectator holding a cigar.

JG: In this choice of a gesture, smoking a cigar, there is a casualness with regard to the work of art that is in fact not permitted. It is not permitted by the work of art. I don't know the Rothschilds, but with the Rothschilds, you can probably talk about art while smoking a cigar. You can't go to the Louvre and look at *The Marquise of Solana*[8] with the same movement as with the Rothschilds who talk about art while smoking a cigar.

HF: So you think that Brecht's gesture is the gesture of a bourgeois capitalist?

JG: Looks like it to me.

HF: At least when looking at a work of art, since you're smoking a cigarillo right now.

JG: If I smoke a cigar as a cigar smoker, if I can be defined as a cigar smoker, if I listen to Mozart's *Requiem* and this gesture of smoking a cigar takes precedence over that of listening to the *Requiem*, then it's not simply a question of distancing, but of a lack of sensibility. It's a question of lacking an ear, which means I would prefer my cigarillo to the *Requiem*.

HF: You were talking about contemplation of the artwork.

JG: I lose more and more the sense of being "myself," the sense of the "I," and become nothing but the perception of the artwork. Confronted with subversive events, my "ego" or my "self," my "social self," is on the contrary more and more filled, it is more and more inflated, and I am less and less capable, when confronted with subversive phenomena, I am less and less free for . . . precisely for that sort of contemplation. One day when he was conducting *Daphnis and Chloe*, I asked Boulez, "I can't tell to what extent your ear registers each instrument," and he said to me . . .

Pierre Boulez said to me, "I can control only about twenty-five or thirty percent," and this is one of the subtlest ears in existence. So someone who is conducting an orchestra has to be immensely attentive, of course, but so does anyone who is listening. Now suppose your ear is less subtle than Boulez's, you have to make such a great effort of concentration that, personally at least, in a museum I can only look at two or three paintings, at a concert I can hear one or two pieces, as for the rest . . . I'm too tired.

HF: And reading?

JG: Oh! It's the same. I can tell you that it took me two months to read *The Brothers Karamazov*.[9] I was in bed. I was in Italy, I would read one page, and then . . . I'd have to think for two hours, then start again, it's enormous, and it's exhausting.

HF: Contemplation absorbs your "self" to the point of destruction?

JG: Not to the point of destruction, not to the point of losing the "self" completely, because at a certain moment, you notice that your leg is asleep, you come back to "yourself," but you tend toward a loss of "self."

HF: Whereas the revolutionary act? ...

JG: In my opinion, it's the opposite, since you have to act. Confronted with the artwork, you have to act, as well. The attention you give to the artwork is an act; if I listen to the vespers of the *Beata Virgine* without at the same time composing it with my own modest means, I'm not doing anything, I don't hear anything; and if I'm not writing *The Brothers Karamazov* while I read it, I'm not doing anything.

HF: So it's double.

JG: Yes. Don't you have the impression that it's kind of like that?

HF: Yes, but revolutionary action is also double.

JG: But it doesn't use the same means. In revolutionary action, you put your body at risk; in the artwork, and in whatever recognition it receives elsewhere, you put your reputation at risk, perhaps, but your body is not in danger. If you botch a poem, if you botch a concerto, if you botch a piece of architecture, people might make fun of you, or you may not have the reputation you deserve, but you aren't in danger of death. When you're involved in revolution, your body is exactly what's in danger, and the whole revolutionary adventure is in danger at the same time.

HF: When you write, is the act of writing closer to that of recreating *The Brothers Karamazov*, is it more like the contemplation of that "thinning out" of the "self," or is it more like the revolutionary act, that concentration of the "self" in physical danger?

JG: The first formula is more accurate. With writing, I never put . . . I have never put my person in danger, or never seriously, in any case. Never in a physical sense. I've never written anything that made anyone want to torture me, put me in prison, or kill me.

HF: But it's a body of work that made an impact and that raised the stakes for an entire generation. It's an exaggeration, but I would say that there isn't a homosexual anywhere in the world now who hasn't been influenced, directly or indirectly, by your work.

JG: First of all, out of simple prudence, I would be wary about what you're saying. It risks giving me an importance that in my opinion I don't have. Second, I think you're mistaken, too; what I wrote did not bring about the liberation you're talking about, it's the other way around: it was liberation that came first and that coincided more or less with Germany's occupation of France and the liberation and peace after the war. It was that kind of liberation and freeing up of minds that allowed me to write my books.

HF: Still, I insist: In Germany, up until 1968, there was a law forbidding sexual acts between adult males. The Genet trial in Hamburg[10] was decisive in securing the freedom to print erotic works, etc.

JG: Even if my books had certain repercussions, the act of writing, the singular act of writing in a prison, had almost no effect on me, so that there is a disproportion between what you're describing, which would be the result obtained by my books, and the writing of my books; the writing, which was pretty much the same if I had described a boy and a girl sleeping together, for me, it was no more difficult than that. I even wonder if there isn't a phenomenon of magnification created by the processes of mechanical reproduction and transmission. Two hundred years ago, if some-one drew my portrait, there would be a portrait. Now, if someone takes a photograph of me—there will be a hundred thousand of them, maybe more; okay, fine, but am I any more important?

HF: No, not more important, but more significant.

JG: But the significance is a new one, it becomes a different one.

HF: When the manuscript of Sade's *120 Days of Sodom* was hid-den in a crack in the wall of the Bastille, it didn't even exist, as Sartre would say; but once it's printed in paperback, it influences an entire population.

JG: Do you think the Marquis de Sade liberated the end of the eighteenth century through his work and his way of living? Personally, I think that, on the contrary, it was the freedom that had begun and was already luminous in the age of the encyclope-dists, in the second half of the eighteenth century, that made Sade's work possible.

HF: Reading your work, one discovers a great admiration for a kind of beautiful brutality, an elegant brutality.

JG: Yes, but I was thirty years old when I wrote my books, and now I'm sixty-five.

HF: And this fascination, which was so bewildering to me, this admiration for assassins, for Hitler, for the concentration camps—all this has drained away?

JG: Yes and no. It has drained away, but the space has not been occupied by anything else, it's a void. It's quite strange for some-one who lives this void. What did it mean, this fascination for brutes or assassins or Hitler? In more direct and perhaps also sim-pler terms, I remind you that I was an orphan, I was raised by Public Welfare, I found out very early on that I wasn't French and that I didn't belong to the village—I was raised in the Massif Central. I found this out in a very stupid, silly way: the teacher asked us to write a little essay in which each student would describe his house. I described mine; it happened that the teacher thought my description was the prettiest. He read it out, and everyone made fun of me, saying, "That's not his house, he's a foundling!" and then there was such an emptiness, such a degra-

dation. I immediately became such a stranger . . . oh! the word
isn't too strong, to hate France is nothing, you have to do more
than hate, more than puke France, finally I . . . and . . . the fact
that the French army, the most prestigious thing in the world thirty years ago, that they surrendered to the troops of an Austrian
corporal, well, to me, that was absolutely thrilling. I was avenged.
But I'm well aware that it wasn't me who wrought this vengeance,
I am not the maker of my vengeance. It was brought about by others, by a whole system, and I'm aware, too, that it was a conflict
within the white world that went far beyond me; but when it
comes down to it, French society suffered a real blow, and I could
only love someone who had dealt such a serious blow to French
society. And then, even as I felt more than satisfied with what had
happened, with the magnitude of the punishment that had been
given to France, that's when, within a few days, the French army
and even much of the French population left, beginning around
the Maubeuge-Basel line[11] almost to the Spanish border. When a
nation is so completely subdued by military force, one has to
admit that France was humiliated, and I can only adore someone
who had wrought the humiliation of France. On top of all this, I
could only place myself among the oppressed people of color and
among the oppressed revolting against the Whites. Perhaps I'm a
Black whose color is white or pink, but a Black. I don't know my
family.

HF: Did the Black Panthers accept you, even though your skin
is white?

JG: Immediately. I wondered about it many times. I was alone,
there were no other whites, I was there with them for two months,
and then the police sent a summons to the Panthers saying I had
to show up at some cop thing.[12] The Panthers said to me, "It's better if you leave, because it might cause some trouble for us." I left.
But for two months, I was alone with them. I ate with them. I
wondered, "Aren't they tired of seeing this white man with them
all the time?" Apparently not. I saw Angela Davis again, three
months ago. I said to her, "We were very afraid for you," and she
said, "We were afraid for you, too." She talked about the moment

during Bobby Seale's pretrial, which I attended,[13] when David
Hilliard, who was replacing Bobby Seale at the time, was arrested.
He was trying to show me a piece of paper, the cops grabbed him
and started taking him away, I saw that he was going to talk and
shout, I said in French, "David, David, don't say anything, be
quiet!" and I was very afraid. I was surprised that no one intervened; I went to find a lawyer there, and I said to him—he had a
beard like yours, and you know American lawyers don't wear
robes—and I took him by the shoulders, I said to him, "Hey, look,
do something . . . stop them . . . " and he had me arrested. I'd
made a mistake, it was the state prosecutor. Since I didn't understand English, I just let them do it; I was arrested, but without any
harsh treatment; they made me leave, but it was almost as if they
were just asking me to leave. What different treatment! I'll tell you
what happened: we entered the courtroom in New Haven. I was
with the Panthers, so there were a dozen Blacks and one White,
me, a sixty-year-old white man, in a tiny courtroom. There were
two or three rows of chairs in the front of the courtroom, then
behind those there were some benches, and in the chairs there
were Whites and on the benches there were Blacks. There happened to be a free seat in the first row of chairs, a cop took me by
the arm and led me, very forcefully, to the free seat, and I went
with him, not understanding what was going on; and it was only
when I looked up before sitting down that I saw David Hilliard
way in the back. I said, "I'll sit with you," and the cop . . . I
knocked him on the hand and said, "Let go," and he did, but you
see, I felt the difference. There was something else: when David
went out, he left behind a little briefcase with some papers in it,
and there was a guy there, a Black, who managed to take it out to
the hallway, but then we had to leave the courthouse. Well, who
did they give the briefcase to? To me, because they knew they
would be searched on the way out of the courthouse and that I
wouldn't be; and that's exactly what happened.

HF: Would you say that the Panthers were carrying out a poetic
revolution?

JG: Hold on! Before saying something like that, I'd like for us to agree about something, if possible. There seem to be at least two kinds of communication: one is a rational, reflective communication. Is this lighter black?

HF: Yes.

JG: Yes. And then there is a communication that is less cer-tain, and yet obvious. I'll ask you if you agree that Baudelaire's verse, "Blue-black hair, a den of taut shadows,"[14] do you find that beautiful?

HF: Yes.

JG: So we're communicating. Okay, there are at least two kinds of communication, then, a mode that is recognizable, controllable, and one that is uncontrollable. The Panthers' action had more to do with the uncontrollable kind of communication. In San Francisco, I was in a taxi driven by a Black man, and I said to him, "Do you like the Panthers?" and he said, "Like them, no; admire them, yes." He was fifty years old, he said to me, "But my kids like them a lot." In reality, he liked them, too. You can't admire something without liking it, but he couldn't say so because he had violent images of them that he rejected. It was claimed that they had ransacked, that they had killed, and that's true, they had killed a few cops, a few Whites. Much less violence, in any case, than the Americans caused in Vietnam and Korea and elsewhere. It was a revolution of an affective and emotional order; and that has no relation . . . well, it may have some very discreet relation to revolutions attempted elsewhere and by others means.

HF: Your conception of revolution would be analogous to that of the Panthers?

JG: No, no, the Panthers put into play an entire affectivity that we lack, and this affectivity did not come from the fact that they were of African descent, that they're black; it's simply that they're banished, they've been banished and outlawed for four centuries, and they found each other again in the expression "brothers." This fraternity is not possible if you're thinking of a global revolution, or so it seems to me. You can't talk about that if don't you have a very long stretch of time out ahead of you.

HF: So we're saying that there is a gap between poetic and artistic revolutions and social revolutions.

JG: What are referred to as poetic or artistic revolutions are not exactly revolutions. I don't believe they change the order of the world. Nor do they change the vision we have of the world. They refine vision, they complete it, they make it more complex, but they don't entirely transform it, the way a social or political revolution does. If during the interview we're going to speak of "artistic revolution," let it be understood between us that we're using an expression that's a little tired, a little lazy. As I said, political revolutions rarely, I might say never, correspond to artistic revolutions. When revolutionaries succeed in completely changing a society, they find themselves faced with a problem: how to give expression, how to express their revolution as adequately as possible. It seems to me that revolutionaries make use of the most academic means they can find within the society they have just overturned or plan to overturn. Everything happens as if the revolutionaries said to themselves, "We're going to prove to the regime we just overturned that we can do as well as they did." And then they imitate the academic styles, they imitate official painting, official architecture, official music. It's only much later that they envisage revolution as a cultural revolution, and then they sometimes appeal not to academic styles, but to tradition and to new forms in which tradition can be used.

HF: Are there no exceptions to this rule? Danton? Saint-Just?

JG: Danton! No. I don't think Danton initiated a revolutionary expression, that is, a new way of feeling and experiencing the world and a new way of expressing it. Saint-Just, perhaps. Not in his proclamations, but in his interventions concerning the death of Louis XVI.[15] The style is still that of the eighteenth century, but with what insolence! The rhythm, the syntax, the grammar, everything belongs to the eighteenth century. But this syntax seems deformed, in any case transformed by the audacity of the positions he takes. You might say that he presented it in a very violent courtly language. But the literature of the time, even Diderot and even sometimes Montesquieu, was quite violent. In his second intervention in favor of the execution of Louis XVI, Saint-Just says: If the king is right and he is the Legitimate Sovereign, then we must kill the people who rose up against him—or else the Legitimate Sovereign is the people, and the king is a usurper, so we must kill the king.[16] That was very new. No one dared to speak so directly.

HF: Over the course of the different French revolutions, are there other moments of poetic or artistic revolution?

JG: No. You see, there was the Paris Commune. In reality, it was the whole Parisian populace that had taken power. Emotionally, that's very beautiful. But the only artist who put himself in the service of a revolution as an artist and at the same time as a revolutionary was Courbet, who was a great painter, but not one who repudiated the painting of his age. Victor Hugo was very proud that a cannon that bore the name Victor Hugo had been cast by the Parisian Foundries. He tried to understand. He understood, more or less, he was even a little terrified by the magnitude of the Paris Commune. But as a writer, he didn't change. Now the Paris Commune seems so short, it lasted so little time, that it was unable to change much. The revolution of 1848? What do we owe to that? Baudelaire was apparently on the barricades, but he had already written the most beautiful poems of *The Flowers of Evil.* *Sentimental Education* came out of the Revolution of 1848. But *Sentimental Education* was written by Flaubert, and Flaubert was not at all in favor of revolution. A new way of feeling that appeared to correspond with the Soviet revolution, at the end of the war, was Surrealism. But then very soon the Surrealists cut their ties both with the Soviet Union—since that was when Aragon wrote "Moscow the Senile"[17]—and with Freud, who misunderstood them. His meeting with Breton made it clear that he was not at all interested in Surrealism and that he did not see psychoanalysis as something to be used for purely poetic ends.

HF: Have you traveled to the Soviet Union?

JG: No, never.

HF: But you were invited to go there?

JG: No. Sartre asked me to go with him;[18] I think he was afraid he'd be bored to death if he went alone; with me there, we would have had a laugh, but I wasn't invited; I probably wouldn't have been able to get a visa.

HF: Why didn't you try?

JG: I was afraid I'd be bored to death.

HF: Do you see in the Cuban experience any chances for a poet-ic and artistic revolution?

JG: No, because when Castro saw the literature and painting of the West, of Europe, he saw them only from Cuba, but they were already recognized forms, they had already become academic, he re-cognized them. But the truly original forms originating in Cuba, he didn't recognize those.

HF: You were supposed to go to Cuba, but you turned that down, too?

JG: When I was invited by the Cuban Cultural Affairs, I said, "Yes, I'd like very much to go to Cuba, but on one condition: I'll pay for my own trip, I'll pay for my stay there, and I'll go where I want and stay where I want," and I said, "I'd like very much to go, if it really is the kind of revolution I'd like to see, that is, if there aren't any more flags, because the flag, as a sign of recognition, as an emblem around which a group is formed, has become a cas-trating and deadly piece of theatricality—and the national anthem? Ask him if there is no longer a Cuban flag and a nation-al anthem." He said, "But you don't understand; our national anthem was written by a Black."

HF: In Cuba there is an idea of death, "Patria o muerte";[19] how do you see that?

JG: It seems very important to me, because, I won't say an artist, but any person takes on his true dimensions once he is dead. That's the meaning, I think, of Mallarmé's line "Such as into him-self eternity finally changes him."[20] Death transforms everything, the perspectives change; as long as a man is alive, as long as he can inflect his thought, as long as, while he lives, he can throw you off track and can try to conceal his true personality by negations or affirmations, you don't really know who you're dealing with. Once he's dead, everything is deflated. The man is fixed, and we see his image differently.

HF: So for you, giving a taped interview is dying a little, fixing something?

JG: No, it's just the opposite, since while I'm talking to you like this I can present an image of myself that's more acceptable, more presentable, according to my desire of the moment. It's hypocritical in a way. When I speak to you, here in front of the microphone, I'm not completely sincere. I want to give a certain image of myself. And I can't say exactly who I am or what I want, because I'm like anyone else, essentially changing.

HF: Do you see in the movement of May '68 the possibility of the kind of revolution you would wish for?

JG: No, no. A lot has been written about May '68, and some have spoken of a "mimodrama," which seems accurate to me. One of the most daring student groups occupied the Odéon theater. I went twice to the Odéon theater when it was being occupied,[21] and the first time there was a kind of violence that was often downright incantatory. Look: the theater and the stage are here; the revolutionaries, a crowd of students were here on the stage. They had more or less reproduced the architecture of an ordinary courtroom, that is, a large table with a spokesman for the Idea behind or in front of it, and on either side the different groups who were challenging or accepting the Idea of the spokesman. Facing them there was the audience, in the boxes and in the seats below, who accepted what they heard, more or less, or who rebelled against it or . . . etc. The second time I went to the Odéon in May '68, all this violence had disappeared; that is, the words that were spoken on the stage were received by the audience—and it really has to be called an audience—and these words, often slogans, came back like an echo from the stage to the audience, from the audience to the stage, more and more feebly each time. In the end, the students had occupied a theater. What is a theater? First of all, what is power? It seems to me that power can never do without theatricality. Never. Sometimes the theatricality is simplified, sometimes it's modified, but there is always theatricality. Power covers and protects itself by means of theatricality. In China, in the Soviet Union, in England, in France, everywhere, theatricality is what dominates. Giscard d'Estaing, for his part, claims that he has destroyed all theatricality; in reality, he replaced the theatricality of the Third Republic with a slightly more modern one in the Swedish or even Canadian style: a procession on foot up the Champs-Élysées,[22] things like that. There is one place in the world where theatricality does not hide power, and that's in the theater. When the actor is killed, well, he gets up, takes a bow, and starts all over again the next day with getting killed, taking a bow, etc. There is absolutely no danger. In May '68, the students occupied a theater, that is, a place from which power has been evacuated, where theatricality remains on its own, without danger. If they had occupied the Parisian law courts, first, that would have been much more difficult, since that building has more guards protecting it than the Odéon theater, but above all, they would have been obligated to send people to prison, to pronounce judgments; then you'd have the beginning of a revolution. But they didn't do that.

HF: Can you say what your political revolution would be like?

JG: No, because I'm not all that eager for there to be a revolution. If I'm really sincere, I have to say that I don't particularly want it. The current situation, the current regimes allow me to revolt, but a revolution would probably not allow me to revolt, that is, to revolt individually. But this regime allows me to revolt individually. I can be against it. But if there were a real revolution, I might not be able to be against it. There would be adherence, and I am not that kind of man; I am not a man of adherence, but a man of revolt. My point of view is very egotistic. I would like for the world—now pay close attention to the way I say this—I would like for the world not to change so that I can be against the world.

HF: Well, what kind of revolution would be the most dangerous for you?

JG: According to what I know about it, the Chinese revolution.

HF: What sort of political revolution is it that you hope for?

JG: First . . . can I take some grapes? I was invited by two revolutionary groups, the Black Panthers and the Palestinians. Okay. I said to you in our previous conversations what was admissible, the admissible reasons; now, what is more difficult to admit has to do with the fact that the Panthers are Black Americans, the Palestinians are Arabs. It would be difficult for me to explain why things are like this, but these two groups of people have a very intense erotic charge. I wonder whether I could have adhered to other revolutionary movements that are equally as just—I find these movements very just, the Panthers and the Palestinians—but isn't this adherence, this sympathy, also driven by the erotic charge that the whole Arab world or the Black American world represents for me, for my own sexuality? And there's something else, the problem of the game. Going to America with the Panthers after the American embassy refused three times to give me a visa, that was a game. I enjoyed myself tremendously, and that's part of it, that too. Even though the work I did there was perhaps very conscientious, I can't say that there wasn't a spirit of provocation on my part; I noticed, for example, that the police either didn't dare to arrest me or didn't know I was there, and, well, the FBI is a joke, it's a complete mess, they don't know who's coming and who's going, or if they do,[23] then ...

HF: They don't give a damn.

JG: They don't give a damn, and, at the same time, there's a very old anti-convict law stating that no person convicted of a crime can be allowed to enter the United States; so they broke their own law.

HF: For me, what emerges from what you call "poetic revolution" are the following points: eroticism, enjoyment, insolence, and perhaps: being in the margins. Is that correct?

JG: Yes. I don't know if it's in the order of priority you chose, but the elements seem to be there; but at the same time with a will to be against all established power, to be on the side of the weakest; because if, not Nixon, but Wallace[24] had invited me to the United States, obviously I wouldn't have gone.

HF: I'm not trying to find contradictions; on the contrary, we understand each other perhaps because we accept contradictions ...

JG: Yes.

HF: You said, as a joke, that you would go to Rome if the Pope invited you.

JG: I said that in a certain situation, in relation to the Cuban invitation; I said that I can't go to venerate Castro like all the European intellectuals have done, but after all, since I don't believe in the Pope, not in the least, the Pope is of no importance at all, and going to Rome would have meant nothing.

HF: Why does the Chinese revolution trouble you?

JG: Because the Chinese revolutionary leaders found a way, first of all, to liberate the immense territory of China from all external powers: the Japanese, the French, the English, the Germans, who else? the Americans, and that seems to me to be extremely significant: all the whites were thrown out; second, and this too is significant, they have fed eight hundred million people, they made it possible for all the Chinese to learn to read and write.

HF: From a very simple point of view: I went to Chile during the time of Allende's government, and it seemed to me that with the political posters, the immense murals that covered entire neighborhoods, in a very different style, every artist could express himself freely, the workers could express themselves freely; they made drawings on the walls, in the streets, in every neighborhood; perhaps it wasn't entirely new, but it created a sense of boisterous energy in an otherwise rather gray Santiago de Chile, and there, for me, was the beginning of a revolutionary pictorial art; how do you see this experiment on the part of Allende's government?[25]

JG: Really, I don't know. What you're saying is new to me, I didn't know about it.

HF: And the economic endeavors of Allende's government, do they seem viable to you?

JG: No, on the contrary, they didn't seem viable to me, if you think of the long series of strikes in the copper mines and by the truck drivers, and the extraordinary inflation, it seemed viable only with great difficulty.

HF: Caused by ITT.[26]

JG: Well, sure, caused by the United States, by ITT, of course, but the government either foresaw it and didn't find the means to remedy it, or else they didn't foresee it.

HF: It seems harsh to hear from you that if the revolutionaries or the students of May '68 had taken over the law courts, they would have had to put other people in prison.

JG: Or destroy the prisons—but in any case, pronounce judgments and executions.

HF: In the case of Saint-Just, it was a question of calling for a death sentence. Is there not, in that audacious and insolent style, the possibility of doing something more progressive than a death sentence?

JG: Oh, of course! The Chinese did it in the case of the former Manchurian emperor; they transformed him into a gardener.

HF: That seems more progressive to you than a death sentence against Louis XVI?

JG: No, more ironic; but in both cases, it's a question of reducing the idea of a man's sovereignty to nothing. Louis XVI was very good with his hands. He was a locksmith, you know. If the French Revolution had made of him a good or an average locksmith, that would have been as beautiful as cutting off his head; but the forces of the moment, during the Terror of 1791 to 1793, were such that he had either to be condemned to death or exiled; and exiling him was very dangerous.

HF: Why is it as beautiful to make someone a gardener or a locksmith as to cut off someone else's head?

JG: It's as beautiful because it means not exalting death, in the case of Louis XVI, but rendering derisory the idea of one man's sovereignty over others.

HF: Is there not for you a certain beauty in the very fact of cutting off someone's head?

JG: In the case of the revolutionaries, I don't know whether one can speak of beauty, because they already had power. And you know, when Pompidou refused to pardon Buffet and Bontemps,[27] the two murderers, it wasn't so beautiful. The murder carried out by Pompidou, the double murder of Buffet and Bontemps, I don't see anything heroic in that, or anything aesthetic, or anything at all. He gave in to public opinion, which clamored for death because the wife of a prison guard was murdered by Buffet. I don't find anything admirable in the fact that he gave in to public opinion.

HF: Whereas the fact that a poor person commits murder, you find that admirable?

JG: First, we mustn't confuse the different perspectives: there is the literary perspective and the lived perspective. The idea of a murder can be beautiful. Real murder, that's something else. Now I saw, really saw, an Algerian murder a Frenchman, just after the Liberation. They were playing cards. I was right there next to them. The Algerian was twenty-four years old, and he had run out of money; the Frenchman had really taken him for a ride. He asked to borrow some money so he could try his luck one more time. He was refused. He took out his knife and he killed. I saw the guy die.[28] That was very beautiful. But why was it beautiful? Because the murder was the culmination, the final endpoint of a revolt that was haunting the Algerian for a long time. It's the revolt that was beautiful, not so much the murder itself. The danger, too, gave it a force, yes . . . in a sense, it made possible a certain conviction, because of the danger involved. The murderer had to run away, and he wasn't captured. For a policeman to kill someone without any risk, no, I don't find that very admirable.

HF: And you, why haven't you ever committed murder?

JG: Probably because I wrote my books.[29]

HF: Have you been haunted by the idea of committing a murder?

JG: Oh, of course! But a murder without a victim. I really do have to make an effort to accept a man's death, even if it's inevitable. So whether it's caused by me, by a normal cessation of the heart, by a car accident, etc., doesn't really matter, it shouldn't really matter, but it does. Now you could ask me the question: have you caused anyone's death?

HF: Okay.

JG: But I won't answer.

HF: Do you mean involuntarily?

JG: No, voluntarily.[30] The question is this: have you voluntarily caused anyone's death?

HF: Okay.

JG: I won't answer.

HF: Has this weighed on you?

JG: No, it hasn't weighed on me at all.

HF: Can you describe the steps in your thinking and the path that led from your life to your written work?

JG: If you will accept a crude answer, I would say that the impulse to murder was diverted into poetic impulses.

HF: How does it happen that we like so much to read about things that are cruel, about murder and torture, that we like to describe murder and torture, and that, in everyday life, we have an extreme reserve toward others, toward the other's body, the integrity of the other?

JG: Can you ask the other corollary question suggested by this one? Why do murderers, when they write, almost always give descriptions of themselves, of their acts, or of their imaginary acts, that sound like First Communion?

HF: You ask that question. I would like to go back to our remarks on the *Iliad.* I think there is something I would call magic, ritual. You touched on it a moment ago when you spoke of theatricality.

JG: I don't agree with you about ritual. What you said the other day, about the formulaic repetition of the same phrases at certain moments, that's not ritual. It's a literary mode of expression that can be used in ritual. Ritual itself is something else. It is the recognition of a transcendence, and it's the repetitive recognition of this transcendence, day after day, week after week, month after month, like the Panathenaea,[31] like the rituals of . . . no, in fact of any ritual, even the rituals of the Catholic Church or Masonic rituals. Books or stories or songs are used for these rituals, but they themselves aren't rituals. The *Iliad* was one of these. During the Panathenaea, the *Iliad* was recited officially. But the *Iliad* itself is neither a ritual nor a sacrament. It's a poem.

HF: But within a world that is very ritualized?

JG: But every world is ritualized. There is no world that is not ritualized, except obviously the most modern research, in laboratories, or ...

HF: Or revolution.

JG: Yes, or revolution, obviously. But only when a revolution is under way, because when it's over, it becomes ritualized almost automatically. Look at everything that happened in China with Mao, all those rituals. Just think, they know, they record every minute and almost every second that Mao Zedong grants to his visitors. Isn't that true?

HF: I'd like to give you a very particular example of ritualization. In certain initiation rites there is a combination of rituals made up of several elements such as flagellation, betrayal of the tribe, betrayal of the family, murder of members of the family, urine rites, excrement rites, rites with animal hides. . . . They are referred to as a "panther society" or a "crocodile society," etc. Rereading part of your work, *Miracle of the Rose* in particular, I see this combination once again, though not within such a narrow circle. Do you think that through your experiences you touched on an archaic and ritual depth?

JG: Yes. Here I don't have any knowledge, I have no knowledge of anthropology. What you just described are rites of passage. The passage from puberty to manhood. There is betrayal of the tribe, but in fact it's in order to reintegrate the tribe. There is drinking of urine, but in fact it's in order not to drink it. With *Miracle of the Rose* in particular, it's possible that I tried to discover some rites of passage on my own, but obviously in an unconscious way. This is an idea that never occurred to me before, but it might explain why I didn't write any more books after I left prison, except *The Thief's Journal.*[32] I didn't have any more to write. The passage was complete.

HF: And that's why your *Oeuvres complètes* were published in 1952?[33]

JG: That's your interpretation. It seems to me to be close to the truth.

HF: What importance does violence have for you?

JG: Oh! We'd have to talk about things I don't know about.[34] We'd have to talk about the potlatch[35] and destructive intoxication. Destructive intoxication even among the most conscious and

intelligent men. Think of Lenin offering the Soviet people public
urinals made of gold. In every revolution there is an intoxicated
panic, more or less contained, but also more or less unleashed.
This intoxication showed itself in France, for example, in all
Europe, by the peasant uprisings before the French Revolution,
and also in other ways; in a ritual or ritualized form in the
Carnival. At certain moments, the entire people wants to be liberated, wants to indulge in the phenomenon of the potlatch, of
complete destruction and total expenditure, it needs violence. I go
to England quite often. I have a lot of admiration for the Rolling
Stones, musically speaking, not for other pop groups, but for the
Rolling Stones, I do. I've been going to England regularly since
1948. And really, almost overnight, at the moment, more or less,
when England lost its whole Commonwealth, all its dependencies,
its whole colonial empire, England at the same time lost its
Victorian morals and it became a kind of bazaar, a party.

HF: Violence and the potlatch are also subject to rules, to
ritualization?

JG: Of course.

HF: All the violence in your work, every catastrophe, is nested
within in a rite. Before he was killed, Pasolini said that proletarian violence has essentially changed, that it tends more toward the
society of consumption than toward anything else, that today,
Italian proletarians kill for things like motorcycles and bourgeois
clothes, and that they need to be punished just like Italian neofas-
cists. I find that conclusion completely false.

JG: Yes, completely false.

HF: But at the same time, do we not see now certain kinds of
gratuitous murder, a derangement of ritual in the fact of killing for
a dollar, a disorder that is absolutely different from the violence
you describe?

JG: But you just said the opposite of what Pasolini said. When
Pasolini says, or said: The function of proletarian violence is to
exert itself for the purpose of appropriating consumer goods. In
fact, I wonder—and you yourself just gave the same answer—if it's
not a question above all of expressing oneself violently, of being

violent and of finding an opening for this violence. It's supposedly for a dollar or for clothes. In reality, it's for the violence itself.

HF: So for you, there's no difference between the violence of *Querelle*[36] and the violence of the young baker who murdered Pasolini?

JG: In the case of the baker, I don't know much about it.[37] I think he may have wanted money or that he was horrified by the idea that Pasolini wanted to screw him or put his hand on his ass. I don't know. With adolescents, anything is possible. They can accept every form of sexuality and the most visible sluttishness, and then suddenly they have to show some sort of heterosexuality. "Hey! I'm a man, I don't want to be touched like that!" I don't know.

HF: Do you believe that the presumed basis of a murder changes its psychological value?

JG: Probably. Man cannot live without justifying himself, and he always finds in his conscience the means and the ability to justify himself and his actions. It's possible that the little baker is sitting in his cell saying to himself, and being encouraged by his lawyer to say to himself and to repeat, "After all, I killed a millionaire who is losing touch with the people, so my cause is just." I don't know, I'm making it up.

HF: Apparently Pasolini had some masochistic tastes.

JG: I don't know the details. If he wanted to be hit or whipped or beaten, it's quite possible that, as a game and because he was paid, the kid struck the first blows, and then soon enough it's the kid himself who is taking pleasure. He can't stop, and he pushes it to the point of killing the guy. That's possible. I don't know.

HF: How do you find the questions I'm asking?

JG: They're good questions, but I can never say the whole truth. I can say the truth only in art.

HF: What is the truth for you?

JG: Before all else, it's a word. It's a word that's used first of all to make someone else believe in your own sincerity. You say: I'm telling you the truth. I don't think I can use this word in an attempt to define it philosophically. Nor can I define it as scientists or scholars do when they speak of an objective truth. Truth is obviously the result of a general observation or observations. But these observations do not necessarily allow one to discover the truth, or, especially, to discover it immediately. Am I going to spend my life or part of my life checking scientific claims?

HF: What scientific claims have you been able to verify?

JG: Practically none.

HF: And which ones would you want to verify?

JG: There is one that intrigues me, namely: Are there races? Does the concept of race mean anything? And are there inferior races and superior races? And if there are superior races, should they have precedence if we don't want humanity to become inferior? But can there even be superior races? That is a truth I would like to know.

HF: For you, the Negro-African would be of a superior race?

JG: Not superior, but not inferior either. Now that requires a demonstration, but I don't have such a demonstration. I know some professors. . . . Well, even the title of professor at the Collège de France doesn't mean very much; they tell me that there are races and that there are inferior races, just as there are inferior and superior individuals, intellectually, physically, etc.

HF: Is there any essential difference between approaching sincerity in a conversation and in art, or is it only a difference of degree?

JG: Here I will answer immediately: yes. There is an essential difference. In art, one is solitary, one is alone before oneself. In a conversation, one speaks with someone else.

HF: And that's disturbing?

JG: Obviously it changes the perspective.

HF: When you write, don't you address yourself to an other?

JG: Never. I probably did not succeed, but my attitude toward the French language is such that I tried to form something with as beautiful a form as possible; the rest was completely indifferent to me.

HF: The language you knew best, or the French language?

JG: The language I knew best, yes, of course, but also the French language, because it was in that language that I was condemned.

The courts condemned me in French.

HF: And you want to answer them on a superior level?

JG: Exactly. There are perhaps other, more subterranean motives, but in the end, I think, they don't come into it very much.

HF: What would they be?

JG: Don't ask me. Ask a psychoanalyst that question, he might be able to answer. Because I think it's very unconscious.

HF: When did you begin to take on this poetic task?

JG: You're asking me to look back in a way that is very difficult, because I don't have many signposts. I think I was around twenty-nine or thirty years old. I was in prison. So that was in '39, 1939. I was alone, in solitary, or in a cell, at any rate. First I should say that I had written nothing except a few letters to friends, both men and women, and I think that the letters were very conventional, I mean full of ready-made phrases I had heard or read, but never really felt. Well, I was going to send a Christmas card to a German friend, a woman who lived in Czechoslovakia. I had bought it in the prison, and the back side of the card, where you're supposed to write, was rough and grainy. And this grain on the card really struck me. Instead of writing about Christmas, I wrote about the texture of the postcard and the snow it evoked for me. That's when I started to write. I believe that was the trigger. It's the trigger I was aware of and able to register.[38]

HF: What were the books and literary works that had impressed you up to that point?

JG: Pulp novels.[39] Novels by Paul Féval. The kind of books you find in prisons. I don't know. Except, when I was fifteen, when I was in the Mettray reformatory,[40] somehow I got hold of a copy of Ronsard's poems, and I was amazed.

HF: And Marcel Proust?

JG: Well, I read the first volume of *Within a Budding Grove* in prison. We were in the prison courtyard and were exchanging books on the sly. It was during the war, and since I wasn't too preoccupied with books, I was one of the last. So somebody said, "Here, you take this one." And I saw the name Marcel Proust. I

said to myself, "This must be incredibly boring." And then. . . .
But here I have to ask you to believe me: if I'm not always sincere
with you, this time I am. I read the first sentence of *Within a
Budding Grove*, which speaks of Monsieur de Norpois, who is
coming to dinner at the house of Proust's parents, or, well, the parents of the one who's writing the book. The sentence is very long.
And when I finished reading that sentence, I closed the book and
said to myself, "Now I can rest easy, I know I'll find one marvel
after another." The first sentence was so dense, so beautiful, and
this adventure was a first great flame announcing a huge inferno.
It took me almost the rest of the day to get over it. I didn't open
the book again until evening, and indeed I found nothing but one
marvel after another.

HF: You had already written one of your novels before reading
Proust?

JG: No, I was still writing *Our Lady of the Flowers*.

HF: Are there other literary works that impressed you as much
as Proust's did?

JG: Oh, of course! Some even more than that. There's *The
Brothers Karamazov*.

HF: And Balzac?

JG: Less so. There's an aspect of Balzac that's somewhat trivial.

HF: Stendhal?

JG: Oh yes, oh yes. Stendhal, of course. *The Charterhouse of
Parma*, and even *The Red and the Black*, but especially *The
Charterhouse of Parma*. But for me, nothing equals *The Brothers
Karamazov*. There are so many different times involved. There was
the time of Sonia and the time of Alyosha, there was the time of
Smerdyakov, and then there was my own time of reading. There
was the time of deciphering, and then there was the time that
came before their appearance in the book. What was Smerdyakov
doing before being spoken of? Finally, I had to put all this together and reconstruct it. But it was very exciting, and very beautiful.

HF: Do you mind if I open a parenthesis on time?

JG: No.

HF: How do you experience time?

JG: You're asking a question that's difficult for me to answer, because for twenty or twenty-five years now, I've been taking Nembutal,[41] and I feel the effects of the Nembutal the entire morning; it makes me sleep almost instantaneously . . . in about ten minutes . . . fifteen . . . yes. But there are effects, for example it's not enough to drink a cup of coffee in the morning. I really have to wait until the Nembutal has stopped affecting my brain. Okay, so during the time when the Nembutal is affecting me, I don't realize how much time is passing. When I have to carry out specific tasks, things that to speak quickly I'll call profane—getting from here to there, buying things—I do them in a very clearcut way, in a very determinate time, I don't get sidetracked. That's no problem. When I want to write, I have to have all my time for myself. I was a little irritated the other day at Gallimard, since I had just seen M. Huguenin,[42] and I asked for a very large sum of money. And Claude Gallimard wanted to give me a monthly payment, a comfortable monthly payment. But I said, "No, I want you to give me everything today." I want to be absolutely free. To sleep when I want. To go where I want. Otherwise, I won't do anything. I won't do anything, it's not possible. I have to be able to stay for two or three days in bed, writing day and night, etc. Or else for only one hour, etc. It depends.

HF: And he refused?

JG: Oh, no, he gave it to me. But then there I was with all these bills that I had to stuff into my pockets.

HF: A monthly payment for a writer, how much is that in France?

JG: I wouldn't know what writers earn. I never asked for details. Since I'm not ashamed of money, of saying how much I earn . . . I couldn't really call it "earning." . . . When I write, there's both a little pain, very little, and a little pleasure. It's not "work." So earn, if you like—well, last year I earned about two hundred thousand francs. And then there are my plays.

HF: Does money itself have any importance for you, the actual bills, etc.?

JG: Yes, especially if they're large. Yes, I like that.

HF: Is money for you a way to gain time, or a way to gain sensuality?

JG: No, not sensuality. Time. I don't earn a lot of money. But I earn enough so that I can dress badly, go without washing, enough to do things like that, to let my hair grow without cutting it, which I don't like to do. Having your hair cut is really a pain in the ass. If my hair isn't cut, it doesn't matter in the least.

HF: There were times when you found yourself on one side of the gulf. Now you're on the other side. How do you feel about the young antisocial people you meet?

JG: I don't feel anything at all. I don't have any guilty feelings. If someone asks me for money (or if I notice, even without being asked), I give it away very easily, really very easily, it doesn't matter to me. There is injustice in the world, but whatever injustice is in the world isn't there because my royalties are relatively high.

HF: You yourself have described scenes in which you robbed pederasts who were looking for sex. Has it ever happened one day that a young man saw you as somebody he might rob?

JG: Yes, that's happened very, very often. It happened in Hamburg, for example, and that time, I couldn't do anything but let the two guys—there were two of them—let them take the money I had in my pockets.

HF: And doesn't that terrify you?

JG: Oh! Not at all, not at all. If it's a lot of money, that bothers me. It makes me angry, because then I have to go back to Gallimard. But you see, I turned fifty-six yesterday . . . fifty-five ...

HF: Fifty-five or sixty-five?

JG: Sixty-five. So I was fifty-six when I was in Karachi.[43] The plane arrived at one in the morning. I was alone. The airport is twenty-five kilometers from the city. So there was a cop who gave me a stamp for a month, and he called a taxi. And I hadn't noticed that the taxi driver was all wrapped in chiffon, and before I could even say no, another guy got in and sat next to me. He was a money changer. He was very insistent. And it was in the middle of the night. "Where are you staying?" he asked me in English. I said, "The Hotel Intercontinental." It's the largest hotel in

Karachi. I said, "Can I exchange ten dollars?" Ten dollars won't get you a room at the Hotel Intercontinental. "I have some friends"—this wasn't true—"I have some friends waiting for me at the Hotel Intercontinental." I didn't want to take the money out. But it was still easy for them to get rid of me after taking everything I had. I stuck to my story. I said, "Listen, that's really all I can give you." He gave me the rupees and then he got out when we got to the Hotel Intercontinental. When we got there, though, the ten dollars weren't enough to pay the young guy. So I asked the porter—the hotel was full, it was nighttime, there were people sleeping everywhere, on chairs, on mats and carpets—I asked him, "Do you have a room? I'd like a room at least for tonight?" "No." What could I do? And my million and a half? It was in a big wad in my pocket all held together with hairpins. To take out one bill I had to take out the whole wad. "Can you exchange some money for me right now?" And I took out all the French money. Suddenly, I had a room. Alright then. But the young guy in the taxi, he didn't know I had all that money, and I gave him a little extra to compensate him. But certainly not as much as he would have gotten if he'd left me stranded fifteen kilometers from Karachi. Now there are also times when I've had good luck: I was in Morocco. I met a young Moroccan,[44] twenty-four or twenty-five, very poor. He came up to my room every day. He stayed in my room. He left my money where it was. He never took anything from me. Do I admire him for that? No. I think it was part of a scheme. But I do admire him for going that far with his scheme.

HF: Later, you brought him to France.

JG: Of course I did, and he was very good at getting what he wanted; I don't regret bringing him to France. In Arab countries, in Third World countries, when a young guy like that meets a white man who shows him a little attention, all he can see is a possible victim, someone to be fleeced; that's just how it is.

HF: What sort of relations could a young man have had . . . a young man who is talented, sensitive, intelligent, who likes men, but is miserable, and who robs an old pederast?

JG: I couldn't tell you. The first thing is that he might just be hungry, and an old pederast would be the easiest person to rob.

HF: When you wrote about that, were you describing yourself?

JG: Yes, of course I did it. I did it in Spain, for example, in Spain, in France. So what?

HF: Didn't you have some perspective, this perspective ...

JG: My point of view, in any case, was that of theft. When I went with a queer, old or not—though I preferred the weakest— it was to steal.

HF: Out of necessity?

JG: Of course, of course.

HF: Didn't it bother you to betray that kind of sexual necessity?

JG: I didn't betray any sexual necessity, I wasn't sexually attract- ed by the old men I robbed; what attracted me was their money; so it was a matter of taking their money, either by knocking them around or by making them come; the only goal was the cash.

HF: Didn't you think that by using an old pederast you were lending a hand to a society that hated you?

JG: Oh, come on. You'd be asking me to be very clear sighted, to have a political and revolutionary consciousness fifty years ago. Fifty years ago, that was around the time of the schism at the Congress of Tours, the birth of the French Communist Party; can you imagine how much any of that could have meant to a fifteen- year-old peasant raised in the Massif Central, what could he have thought? That was the great epoch of Rosa Luxemburg;[45] do you really think I could have thought about that? You can think it now.

HF: When did you discover that you had inclinations for men?

JG: I was very young. Maybe eight years old, nine at the most, in any case, very young, in the country and at the Mettray refor- matory, where homosexuality was condemned, of course; but since there weren't any girls, there was no other choice. All the boys were between fifteen and twenty-one years old; there was no recourse except in a fleeting homosexuality, and that's what made it possible for me to say that in the reformatory I was truly happy.

HF: And you knew you were happy?

JG: Yes, I certainly did. Despite the punishments, despite the insults, despite the blows, despite the poor living and working conditions, despite all that, I was happy.

HF: Did you realize that this behavior was different from that of other people?

JG: No, I don't think the question ever occurred to me. At the time, it was rare for me to ask myself any questions at all about other people. No, for a very long time my attitude remained narcissistic. It was my happiness, it was own happiness that concerned me.

HF: Did you stand out?

JG: Yes, I stood out. First of all because—though you may think I'm contradicting myself—despite the very profound and solemn happiness I experienced being in this home and having such warm relations with other boys of my age, or a little older, or a little younger, I don't know, I wasn't aware of any protest against this regime and the penal regime, the social regime. Just imagine, it was only when I left, when they let me out to go join the army, that I found out about Lindbergh crossing the Atlantic.[46] I didn't know about it. I didn't know about things like that. You're isolated, you're completely cut off from the world. It's like a convent. Well, my own protest was much harsher and more ferocious than that of the toughs, for example. I think I understood very quickly how to make everyone see what was derisory in this attempt at reeducation and in the prayer sessions, since we had to pray, the gym sessions, the little flags for good conduct, all that nonsense.

HF: Did this consciousness extend to erotic life and sexual encounters? Or did you accept, within the world of the prison, the roles that the system laid out for you?

JG: No. But I never experienced sex in its pure state. It was always accompanied by tenderness, perhaps a very quick and fleeting affectivity, but until the end of my sexual life, there was always . . . I never made love in a void. . . . I mean without some affective content. There were individuals, young guys, individuals . . . but no role. I was attracted by a boy my age. . . . Don't get me caught up in definitions. . . . I can't define what love is, of course . . . but I could only make love with boys I liked, otherwise . . . I also made love with some guys to make money.

HF: Do you have a revolutionary concept of eroticism?

JG: Oh no. Revolutionary! No. Spending time with Arabs has made me . . . has happily satisfied me in general. In general, young Arabs are not ashamed of an old body, an old face. Growing old is a part . . . I won't say of their religion, but it's part of Islamic civilization. You're old; you're old.

HF: Has being older changed your relations with your Arab friends?

JG: No. I understand them better. When I was eighteen, I was in Syria,[47] I was in love with a little barber in Damascus. He was sixteen, I was eighteen. . . . And everybody, in the street at least, everybody knew that I was in love with him, and they laughed, well, the men did, the women wore veils and were never to be seen . . . but the other boys, the young people, and older, too, smiled about it and made jokes. They said to me, "Well go ahead, go with him." And he himself was not at all embarrassed. I know he was sixteen. So I was eighteen and a half, more or less. . . . And I felt very comfortable with him. Very comfortable with his family, very comfortable with the city of Damascus. I was in Damascus not long after the bombing that followed the revolt of the Druses, ordered by General Goudot. . . . General Gouraud[48] . . . this guy was missing an arm, and he had transformed Damascus into a pile of ruins. He had fired cannons, and we had strict orders always to move around with a weapon and in groups of three, and we had to keep to the sidewalk. If any Arabs, or anyway any Syrians, women or old men, passed by or came toward us, they were the ones who had to step down off the sidewalk. This rhythm was broken, it was broken by me—and only in my case, naturally. I always stepped aside for women, and I went into the souks, which were wonderful in Damascus. I went into the souks without a weapon, and they found out soon enough, because in Damascus there were maybe two hundred, two hundred fifty thousand people living there, and I was very warmly welcomed.

HF: In your life now, is there a sort of fatherliness that comes into play in your relations with younger men?

JG: Oh yes! But despite myself. It's their doing, not mine.

HF: Would you like to give them a certain security in daily life or open the way to art for them?

JG: Of course. This is a very old and complicated problem you're bringing up. Today you're asking me personal questions, but it happens that I've reached a point in my life where my person doesn't count for much. I don't think I want to hide anything, it's simply that it bores me. You're trying to touch on my problem in its singularity, but my singular problem no longer exists.

HF: But your obsessions, your feelings and resentments, have been projected out into the world. They have had an influence on the behavior of a whole generation.

JG: Maybe. But you're talking about things that happened thirty-five or forty years ago and that have been more or less blotted out by age, by memory, by the drugs I've taken, one of their effects being precisely to blot out from memory everything that might be unpleasant and to leave behind only what's pleasant. And you're reminding me of a world of virgin forest that may still exist, but in which I no longer live in the same way. The virgin forest certainly exists, but I have pruned the largest branches from it. I've made for myself a sort of clearing; I can no longer see the primordial forest very clearly. And when you say to me, "But there where you live, there were ferns, there were creepers"—okay, if you say so, I know it's true, but what they were like I don't know anymore. It doesn't interest me very much. All that has withered away.

HF: What is your theory of homosexuality?

JG: I don't have one. Or I have several. Several have been worked out. None is satisfactory, whether it's the Oedipal theory of Freud, the genetic theory, or Sartre's theory about me in one of his books. He says that I responded in a certain way, but freely, to the social conditions in which I found myself, but that doesn't satisfy me, either. In the end, I don't know. I don't have a theory of homosexuality. I don't even have a theory of an undifferentiated desire. I say: I'm homosexual. Okay. There's not much to it. Trying to find out why or even how I became homosexual and how I realized it, why I am, is a pointless diversion. . . . It's a little bit like trying to understand why my eyes have green pigmentation.

HF: In any case, it's not a neurosis, in your opinion?

JG: No. In fact, I wonder if I didn't experience it as the resolution of a neurosis, if there wasn't a neurosis that came before homosexuality. But of course, I can't say for sure.

HF: Isn't it striking to you that, in all the revolutionary models that we know, there is no freer theory of sexuality than the petit-bourgeois theory of sexuality?

JG: One has the impression in the end that revolutions are carried out by family men.

HF: When you were with the Palestinians and the Black Panthers, were you accepted as a homosexual?

JG: It's very funny. An American television program came to tape me with David Hilliard, there was a Black who was asking questions, and he said to David, who obviously knew since he was reading all my books—he kept them in his bag—he said to him, "Do you know that Jean Genet is homosexual?" David said, "Yes, what about it?" "It doesn't bother you?" "No; if all the homosexuals would come eight hundred miles to defend the Panthers, that wouldn't be bad."

HF: He's being nice; there's no substance behind it. Imagine a good socialist, a real womanizer, Castro, for example ... [49]

JG: His brother is homosexual. Raoul Castro. So people say.

HF: Let's suppose that a good socialist, handsome, powerful, a womanizer, shows up at the Panthers'. They probably wouldn't go so far as to serve as a procurer for him, but they would casually help him, they might even introduce him to some women. To accept in a revolutionary way the homosexuality of Jean Genet in the midst of the Black Panthers would have made it livable, it would have made it concrete.

JG: Well, listen. David liked women. He was married, but he also had women on the side. But I know that a Black, and I don't think he was homosexual, one evening after I had spoken at Yale University—we were always embracing, everyone would embrace me, and he didn't embrace me like the others, but very affectionately, he really squeezed me, and he wasn't . . . and he didn't try to hide it, either. He did it in front of twenty Blacks.

HF: You spoke a moment ago about the end of your sexual life; did your fascination, your desire not go any further with the Black Panthers?

JG: What they asked of me was really very, very difficult. I was still taking Nembutal, since I had to sleep. These were young guys, from eighteen to twenty-five years old, maybe twenty-eight. David was twenty-eight, he had an extraordinary energy. He would wake me up at two in the morning, I'd have to go give a press conference, at two in the morning, and I had to be awake and ready to respond to the questions. Believe me, I wasn't thinking about making love. And then there was another phenomenon, which is that I didn't make any distinctions between the Panthers, I loved them all, I wasn't attracted by one rather than another. I loved the phenomenon of the Black Panthers. I was in love with that.

HF: So you weren't imposing on yourself an erotic abstinence that in a more liberal world you would not have accepted?

JG: Not at all. To the point that Bobby Seale had sent me a letter asking me to write an article on homosexuality; and this letter was either badly translated or carelessly written, in any case I answered saying, "If you attack homosexuals, I'll attack the Blacks." The next week I received a copy of the newspaper, Newton himself had written an article in which he said that it was absolutely necessary to be on the side of the homosexuals, that it was necessary to defend them, that they were a minority group, and that it was necessary to accept their help in defending the Panthers and at the same time to accept defending them.[50]

HF: Are you sure this defense would really have been put into practice?

JG: Obviously I have no proof. No, I'm not sure. Because the Panthers were very young as a movement, I met them in 1970, so the movement was only two years old. They said they didn't believe in God, but they wanted to get married in churches, things like that. So ...

HF: I would like to go back to the question of your literary creation. Were there other important readings that went alongside the creation of your novels?

JG: Dostoyevsky.

HF: Already in prison?

JG: Yes, oh yes. Before going to prison. When I was a soldier, I read *The House of the Dead*, I read *Crime and Punishment*. For me, Raskolnikov was a man who was alive, more alive, much more alive than Léon Blum, for example.

HF: When you left prison, you found yourself surrounded by the literary world. You became friends with Cocteau; he defended you, I believe?

JG: Yes, but that belongs to a little pseudoliterary story of no interest, of no importance at all.[51]

HF: Do you respect Cocteau as a poet?

JG: No. You know, my poetic apprenticeship is very limited. There's Baudelaire, Nerval, Rimbaud, I think, that's all.

HF: Mallarmé?

JG: Oh yes! Of course, Mallarmé.

HF: Not Ronsard?

JG: No, no, no.

HF: Rutebeuf? [Satiric French poet of the thirteenth century known for his biting social commentary—*Trans.*]

JG: Yes, but it's sporadic with Rutebeuf. There are verses by Mallarmé I know by heart, by Baudelaire, Nerval, Rimbaud, I can recite them by heart, but not Rutebeuf.

HF: You're preparing a new work; will it be a work for the theater?

JG: I can't talk about that. I don't know what it will be.[52]

HF: Did I annoy you today?

JG: You didn't really annoy me. The questions you asked were less interesting than the ones you asked yesterday and the day before. Today you wanted me to speak of myself. I'm not all that interested in myself anymore.

HF: Still, do you think that the interview gives an idea of what you really think?

JG: No.

HF: What's missing?

JG: The truth. It's possible when I'm alone. Truth has nothing to do with a confession, it has nothing to do with a dialogue; I'm speaking of my truth. I tried to answer your questions as closely as I could. In fact, I was very far away.

HF: That's very harsh, what you're saying!

JG: But harsh for whom?

HF: For anyone who tries to approach you.

JG: I can't say anything to anybody. To others, I can't say anything but lies. If I'm all alone, I speak a bit of the truth, perhaps. If I'm with someone else, I lie. I'm somewhere else, off to the side.

HF: But lies have a double truth.

JG: Yes! Try to discover the truth they contain. Try to discover what I wanted to hide by saying certain things to you.

TRANSLATED BY JEFF FORT

# § 12    Chartres Cathedral, A "Bird's-Eye" View

Two poles: Chartres and Nara,[1] poles of an axis around which the Earth turns. We chance almost at random on Chartres. Chartres in the Beauce.

The two shrines are immediately evoked in order to open a discussion later on concerning the "right to difference."[2]

Few things remain in our memories or in specialized books, and nothing at all on the Beauce plain, of its first-century inhabitants or of their dwellings. Our Lady of Chartres remains. Breathtaking. In Japan, the shrines of Nara remain.

For what follows, Chartres was not chosen with great effort. Nor was Nara. I had them, so to speak, at hand, but at each place on the planet an axis crossing it ends: two poles of equal value.

The builders of cathedrals were foreigners come from the construction sites of Burgos, Cologne, Brussels: foremen, figure carvers, stonecutters, manufacturers of stained-glass windows, alchemists of enamel ...

—We're about to go stand in front of *The Tree of Jesse*[3]—those numerous foreigners were building a church that would be French, then. Muslims were maybe there for a part of it, small or great, Toledo only a few weeks away by horseback.

Hands, and minds, worked a lot. We have no record of wall posters, around 1160, asserting the value of manual labor.[4] That may be because the stonecutter—to take that example—at first hewing the stones coarsely, tried to copy the figure carvers a little, and his joy was great when he completed the first leaf of ivy that, along with others, would form the band encircling the nave at Amiens. No longer a stonecutter, he is a sculptor. It is not inconceivable, then, that some stoléru[5] taught him that manual labor is a servitude from which he could extricate himself through intellectual investigation. That is how he little by little invents those different methods of leverage that, lessening his pain, led him to the posters revalorizing the exhausting labor he had just had the weakness to relinquish ...

The nave at Chartres is today French and a national—worse, cultural—jewel. But the chapter that decided on its coming into the world was made up, like the construction team, of men from all over.

Vagabonds, probably, more or less well-organized in heterogeneous bands, rather than settled workshops, built what remains— the most beautiful thing that remains in France, especially there, and that official France brags about possessing.

Those men from all over of course did not make up the core of the Chartres population, nor did they mix with the already existing core. They will go on to work and die anywhere at all.

A country is not a fatherland [*patrie*]. It is highly unlikely that a region could be a fatherland naturally made up of men and women who, having the same values, would have greater equality with one another and would know each other better. If France, with all its regions, were a chocolate Easter egg full of little chocolate eggs, each egg would not be a fatherland.

Let us take up the old-fashioned word "affinity." Men who have the same affinities are not in the same chocolate egg. Lovers of Chartres and Nara are as numerous in Morocco, in South Africa, in Germany, in Greece, in Japan, in Holland, in all the nations of the world, even, as in France or Beauce.

*The Tree of Jesse* is the theme of the central panel of the royal portal. Instead of the Italian Mona Lisa, the minister, [André] Malraux, could have sent *The Tree of Jesse* to Japan for an exhibition, the sudden levitation of contemporary and ancient works of art placed into orbit around the globe would have made it possible.[6]

If extreme mobility is a sign of modernity, why not send, whole and by air, Chartres cathedral to spend almost a year in Tokyo? And not its life-sized replica in polyester, since the sky is full of so many works of art that take the plane from one country to another—Tutankhamen. Matisse. Van Gogh, Etruscan art, Pierre Boulez, The Apocalypse of Angers, take world tours several times a year.

To whom does *The Tree of Jesse* belong? Undoubtedly to the people of Beauce, who found it there at the foot of the cradle, and who never saw it.
Just as the Turks own the Venus de Milo.

Is Chartres cathedral French, Beauce, or Turkish?

Perhaps the region should bring a little fatherland into the big one and so permit each Frenchman to have two of them—because as it is, he's the only one in the world who can't pronounce this grandiose asininity: "Every man has two fatherlands, his own and France."[7]

No longer will Pharaonic civilization, despite the recent restorations of Rameses II, despite the ridiculous royal salute accorded to two wooden crates containing his mummy cut in two,[8] be able to recognize itself in Sadat's Egypt, nor ancient provinces in the new administrative districts.

If these districts are to move us, for them to tremble or smile at us, we will have to appeal to the dead provinces.

If every man has a value equal to every other man, every corner of the earth, even the most barren, is worth every other—hence, I hope I'll be forgiven, my total detachment with regard to any particular region, but hence, too, my emotion sometimes when I am faced with what has been abandoned. To keep my interest, it had better be scrap.[9]

Without building a cathedral, every nomad—the Sahraoui[10] for instance—loves the stony corner where he has put up his tent and that he will leave. Pitching camp and breaking camp [*foutre le camp*], hope and slight heartbreak mixed together.

The fatherland is not a nation. At best, it can be a threatened nation, an ill nation, a wounded or troubled nation.

France was certainly a fatherland for many during the first weeks of the Exodus [of 1940]. For the five years that followed, it was fatherland for many fewer Frenchmen.

If danger disappears or if only its theatricality dissolves, the nation becomes again the piece of a more delicate administrative wheel.

One can still wonder if the multiplicity of media might not be more efficient for the rapid, true, smooth functioning of an increasingly complex society.

Each region already does its own things. Like the southern ones that, every morning, polish and shine their sun. To every stranger who sounds Parisian, they explain how they have formed, chiseled, polished, labored on the sun, and how before they came, there lived, in night and fog, shivering populations who died of cold and tuberculosis.

—"But our hot sun cures everything ..."

I repeat, without knowing why, that a homeland can be known as a homeland only in the misfortunes that come from elsewhere.

Obviously, each one of us is tempted to go carry misery elsewhere.

Virtues of the soil. Happiness of being at home, on one's ground.

Desire for the underground: appropriation of ground for the exploitation of those underground by the grasping foreigner.

The homeland is on the pellicular surface of the ground—thanks to its deep foundations, to its superimposed crypts, Chartres cathedral doesn't risk yielding the plain to the wheat fields.

When they intone, at their work tables, the beautiful names of French villages, poets must have a sardonic grin. This thousand-year-old country smells of the stake: Albi, Montségur, Rouen, Nantes, Paris. . . . And of decay: the hanged men of Bretagne, the drowned men of Nantes—again!—the besieged of La Rochelle . . . So?

Where and how were the union and unity of France made, in what places? Let us not forget the little Bretons, Basques, Corsicans, Alsatians, Picards, Normans, who discovered they were French in Algiers, Tannanarive, Hanoi, Timbuktu, Conakry ...

Our zouaves and our marines were there.

They returned to the metropolis to be more equal among themselves, to have the same rights and values, able to look each other in the eye at the same level. Rights of free men, obviously.

Royal France was made by iron, by fire, in all the burnings inside France—with one exception but a considerable one—the Crusades.

Bourgeois France was made by iron, by fire, in burnings and in France Overseas.

The day before yesterday the world. Today the region. Tomorrow Europe.

It seems we have been perceiving the breathing of a being we thought less alive: the ideal sphere is inflated, stretched, and directed toward one single government. It inhales. And everything retracts, breaks up, cracks into tiny fatherlands. It exhales.

For years, we have felt that all men were alike. Today, we pretend to believe in the "right to difference" for the peoples of "over there."

Yesterday, under blinding differences, we discovered the almost ungraspable sameness of our fellow creatures; today, by administrative decree, we dissolve that sameness so that difference can above all be manifest.

In the name of this "right to difference," let us protect the spirituality of India. The wretchedness of Calcutta is nothing compared to it. And let us protect the innocence of Africa. At least may our fat-men's spirituality find itself in the death wards of Dacca[11] and our innocence in the barbed wire of Djibouti. From afar, let us admire the transparency of those who disembody themselves for us.

And Chartres inside? And *The Tree of Jesse*? And Nara in Japan? And our cultural gifts—expensive missiles with a weak impact: really it's not much when we know that, despite "that," an Arab in Paris will have no real peace except in his wretched douar,[12] his true homeland.

Each nation has its own spirit, yes; so what? Each country, in fact, has "its right to difference," so what?

And each region its own.

All the provincial conscripts, from Charles X to Poincaré, after having taken part in brutal conquests over a great part of the world, after having stretched around the earth the red sash of the French Empire, their sons and their grandsons experienced the backwash. Maybe it's up to the French Left to undertake the opposite of bourgeois republics.

We shouldn't reproach the men of yesterday with anything. Let today's men act differently. Real fidelity is often to do the opposite of those to whom one vows fidelity.

Perhaps we should expect something else of the Left besides a well-moderated arrangement of French territory, expect it, rather, to discover, to lay bare this: that "sameness" and "difference" are two words to indicate one single mode of the real.

We must not allow the "right to difference" to let a thousand men die of hunger. With or without new regions, the French can live, but not the Palestinians, Bengalis, Sahraouis, not yet. The picturesque quality of the world—of the Third World surviving in a high Middle Age—camouflages similarity and even sameness.

Cuban soldiers helping Angola,[13] that was a beautiful manifestation of the Left in the world.

If the idea of modernity has any meaning, it is because of the mobility of the age. But one could say that nostalgia is an element of man and that it is prudent to have one's country house, one's countryside, one's land, one's territory, however restricted it may be. Maybe? Do we want to leave in order to come back? Or only to know that an intangible place exists?

I'll sum up: a more or less Saxon chapter, or one more or less impregnated with Latinity and Christian myths, bathing in paganism in which Fairies and the Virgin are confused, the chapter of Chartres ordering troupes of stonecutters, vagabonds, but talented, brilliantly uses the ribbed vault, then the ogival arch, in the midst of an unsophisticated populace and pious whores whose wages are used to pay for the stained glass, on the other side of the world from it rice planters around Nara, the two peoples had much in common, their smile, laughter, tears, fatigue, and they also have the right to difference.

# § 13 "*The Brothers Karamazov*"

Artistic or poetic works of art are the highest form of the human spirit, its most convincing expression: that is a commonplace that should be filed under the rubric "eternal truth." Whether they are the highest form of the human spirit, or the highest form given to the human spirit, or the highest form taken, patiently or quickly, by a lucky chance, but always boldly, it is a question of a form, and this form is far from being the limit to which a human can venture.

Let us go to Dostoyevsky, or rather to *The Brothers Karamazov*, masterpiece of the novel, a great book, a bold instigation of souls, excess, and excesses. This is how I think about it too, and add a wish to laugh in the face of the false and very real imposture that determines the destiny of this book. Dostoyevsky at last completes something that would make him supreme: a farce, a piece of buffoonery at once enormous and petty, and since it is exercised over everything that made him such a possessed novelist, it is exercised against himself, and with shrewd and childlike methods, which he uses with the stubborn bad faith of Saint Paul.

If he carried this novel inside himself for more than thirty years, it is possible that he wanted to write it seriously, that is to say, like *Crime and Punishment* or *The Idiot*, but in the course of writing, he must have smiled, perhaps first at one of his techniques, then at Dostoyevsky the novelist, and finally he must have let himself be carried away by jubilation. He was playing a good trick on himself.

Knowing little about the techniques of composing novels, I still don't know if a writer begins a book with its beginning or with its end. In the case of *The Brothers Karamazov*, I find it impossible to see if Dostoyevsky wanted to begin with the visit of the Karamazov family to the starets Zossima, but even if I had to wait for the death and stench of the starets, from that moment on, I was on the track of something.

Everyone expects a miracle: the opposite happens; instead of a corpse remaining intact, which would be the least to ask, the corpse stinks. So, with a sort of delicious relentlessness, Dostoyevsky does everything to disconcert us; we wait for Grushenka to be a bitch: at Katya Ivanovna's, Alyosha first sees a beautiful young woman, *seemingly* very good and generous, and in her enthusiasm, gratitude, and tenderness, Katerina Ivanovna kisses his hand. Shocked, Grushenka in turn brings Katerina Ivanovna's hand to her mouth, breaks out laughing, and insults her rival. Humiliated, Katerina chases Grushenka away.

When Alyosha returns to the monastery, the starets's corpse smells worse and worse; windows had to be opened. Alyosha goes out. At night, he throws himself on the ground, kisses the earth. He even claims to have experienced a visitation at that moment, and he ends up, with his monk's robe, in Grushenka's apartment.

What allows Alyosha to remain pure, we know, is his smile on all occasions when someone else in his place would be disturbed: when he is still a monk, Lisa sends him a note, and, determined to marry her, he smiles and quite seriously consents to become her husband. Later on, when the boy Kolya tells him, "in brief, Karamazov, you and I are in love with each other," Alyosha blushes a little, and agrees. Alyosha smiles, he is twenty years old. A similar amusement, at the age of sixty, makes Dostoyevsky smile: one gesture or another can be interpreted as one likes. The Prosecutor at the trial explains Dmitri Karamazov's motives, and the lawyer, just as shrewd, gives them an opposite meaning.

Every action has a meaning and an opposite meaning. For the first time, it seems to me, the psychological explanation is destroyed by another (opposite) psychological explanation. The actions or intentions that we have a habit—in books and even in daily life—of considering as wicked lead to salvation, and kindly acts and intentions provoke catastrophe. Kolya raises a dog that little Ilyusha thought he poisoned or killed with a pin. Ilyusha, having fallen ill, hopes only that when Kolya arrives and the dog returns, Kolya may finally visit Ilyusha and bring the dog: Ilyusha's joy is so great that he dies of it.

Ivan Karamazov's dilettante, sure-of-himself attitude makes Dmitri hurl words and even deeds at his father; they lead him to Siberia.

At the beginning of the trial, Ivanovna speaks warmly about Dmitri; fifteen minutes later, she reads a letter from Dmitri to the court: Dmitri is condemned.

Dostoyevsky shows hostility toward socialism, and even toward psychology.

Against socialism he is fierce (see the scenes in which Kolya, by his behavior, ridicules socialism), but once again, the seed must die: it is a socialist revolution that permits millions of Russians to read Dostoyevsky today.

As to psychology, he handles it well: unlike his other novels, where he gives only a straightforward explanation of motives, here, he will also give the opposite explanation: with the result, for the reader, that everything—characters, events, everything— means this *and* also its opposite, nothing is left but tatters. The fun begins. Both ours and the novelist's. After each chapter, we're sure: there's no truth left. And a new Dostoyevsky appears: he clowns around. He amuses himself by giving a *positive* explanation of events, and then as soon as he perceives that this explanation is true in the *novel*, he offers the opposite explanation.

Masterly humor.[1] Game. But risky, because it destroys the *dignity* of the narrative. It's the opposite of Flaubert, who sees only *one* explanation, and the opposite of Proust, who heaps up explanations, who posits a great number of motives or interpretations, but never demonstrates that an opposite explanation is permissible. Did I read *The Brothers Karamazov* badly? I read it as a joke. With affirmation, and worthily, Dostoyevsky destroys preconceptions about what a work of art should be with this book.

It seems to me, after this reading, that every novel or poem or painting or piece of music is an imposture if it does not destroy itself, I mean does not construct itself as a carnival duck shoot, where it is one of the heads we aim at.

They talk a lot these days about laughing at the gods. The work of art constructed on assertions alone, which are never questioned, is an imposture that hides something more important. Frans Hals must have laughed a lot with *The Women Regents* [*of the Haarlem Almshouse*] and *The Regents* [*of the Old Men's Almshouse*]. Rembrandt, too, with the sleeve of *The Jewish Bride*.[2] Mozart, composing his *Requiem* and even *Don Giovanni*. Everything was allowed them. They were free. Shakespeare, too, with *King Lear*. After having had talent and genius, they know something rarer: they know how to laugh at their genius.

And Smerdyakov?

Because there are four of them, the three brothers Karamazov. The gentle Christian Alyosha doesn't say a single word, doesn't make one gesture, to show that this worm is his brother.

I'd like to talk about Smerdyakov.

# Appendix: Background Notes on "Interview with Hubert Fichte," "Chartres Cathedral, a 'Bird's-Eye' View," and *The Brothers Karamazov*

*by Albert Dichy*

## Interview with Hubert Fichte

Interview conducted December 19, 20, and 21, 1975, in Paris, for the German newspaper *Die Zeit.* The present text is based on the typed transcript corrected by the author and published in facsimile by Éditions Qumran.

### INTRODUCTORY NOTE

In 1975, the political activity that had dominated Genet's life since around May 1968 began to subside. Forbidden to enter Jordan, he also saw the dissolution of the Black Panther movement in the United States and the slow settling of the great wave of protest that had risen in France a decade earlier. Genet set to work, attempting to give form to the mass of notes, stories, and memories he had written down, during his travels of the previous five years, on loose sheets of paper, hotel stationery, or in the children's school notebooks he often used. A "great revolutionary and romantic song" was announced in the press (*Playboy*, French edition, no. 24, November 1975, p. 14).

However, in September, after looking over his first attempts to put the text in order, Genet was discouraged by what he saw and became convinced that he had not yet found the form or the key to the work he was dreaming of; he suspended work on the project for the time being and renounced all publication.

Cut off from his literary project, disengaged from the grip of political activity, Genet found himself doubly idle. It was just then that Hubert Fichte, a German novelist and journalist who wanted to conduct a long interview with him for *Die Zeit*, managed to make contact with Genet after five months of fruitless efforts. Thanks to the friendships he had established at Éditions Gallimard, where his latest novel, *Puberty*, was due to appear, Hubert Fichte arranged an interview with Genet for the purpose of proposing and explaining his project. The first meeting took place on December 18, 1975, in the office of Laurent Boyer, Genet's contact at Gallimard. Despite his reluctance, the writer was quickly convinced by Fichte's arguments and perhaps even more by his enthusiasm; in accepting, he also indicated to Fichte the general topics he wanted to discuss.

The interview took place over the course of three meetings, on December 19, 20, and 21, in Hubert Fichte's room at the Hôtel Scandinavia, at 21 rue de Tournon. Several photographs of Genet were taken by Leonore Mau, who accompanied Fichte; these would be used to illustrate the various publications of this text (and in particular, the first full edition, published by Qumran).

Genet found in Fichte a true interlocutor, and whether it was because of Fichte's personality (the forty-year-old Hubert Fichte was both an established novelist and a noted anthropologist specializing in religions of African origin found in the Americas), his own momentary availability, or the distance that now separated him from his recent political experiences, rarely did Genet ever express himself so freely as he does here. Nowhere else—with the exception of *Prisoner of Love*—does Genet display the diversity of his interests and the breadth of his knowledge in fields as varied as architecture, music, anthropology, and history. Genet stops here to take his bearings; he evokes his childhood; he addresses the problem of homosexuality, as well as the complex relation between the political and the erotic.

After the interview was recorded, Hubert Fichte took the tapes back to Hamburg. On January 23, 1976, he sent a typescript of the French transcription, together with a German translation, to Laurent Boyer, who sent them on to Genet. Genet carefully reread the text and made a few minor changes: he added a few relatively brief interpolations and eliminated parts of certain sentences, but mostly he corrected linguistic errors and awkward expressions while also preserving the oral quality of the text.

On February 13, 1976, excerpts from the interview appeared in *Die Zeit* (no. 8, pp. 35–37) under the title "Ich erlaube mir die Revolte" [I allow myself to revolt]. A subtitle was added: "A Scandalous Poet—Interview with Jean Genet." Some biographical information was included with the article, stating that while Genet is "probably one of the greatest poets of the century," he is "certainly the most scandalous."

The interview attracted a great deal of attention and was soon published a number of times, often on Fichte's own initiative, both in large newspapers and in homosexual magazines (Richard Webb, in *Jean Genet and his Critics*, mentions the publication of excerpts that same year in Hamburg in *Him* and *Applaus*.)

Excerpts from the interview were soon translated and published outside Germany: in London in April 1977, in issue 37 of *New Review*; in the United States in 1978, in issue 35 of *Gay Sunshine*; in Spain in February 1982, in *Chimera*; etc.

Genet had authorized Fichte to use the interview as he wished, under two conditions: the text was to be published neither in French nor as a separate volume. However, in the first months of 1981, a work consisting of a facsimile of the typescript in both languages, including Genet's corrections (for the French) and those of Fichte (for the German translation), appeared in Frankfurt, put out by Éditions Qumran (in the Portrait series). It bore no other title than the names of the authors: Fichte, Genet.

Infuriated by the publication, Genet nevertheless decided not to take any legal action against the small publishing house.

A few months later, the entire interview was published for the first time in France by Jean-Pierre Dauphin and Pascal Fouché in *Magazine littéraire* (no. 174, June 1981), and was reprinted several times. It was also published as a separate volume in Italy in March 1987 (Ubulibri, Milan).

TRANSLATED BY JEFF FORT

SOURCES: Interviews with Laurent Boyer and Friedrich Fleming. Archives of Gallimard, Qumran.

## Chartres Cathedral, A "Bird's-Eye" View

Article published June 30, 1977 in *L'Humanité*. We are preserving here the typographical layout of the original.

BACKGROUND NOTES

On June 30, 1977, this text on Chartres cathedral appeared as first in a series of daily chronicles in the cultural pages of *L'Humanité*, a series that became rather successful. Entitled "Lire le pays" [Reading the country], it offered, as Charles Silvestre remarked in his brief introduction, "writings on the provinces, biographical narratives linked to place, a poem about the city, fables about tourist sites."

Each day throughout the summer, a writer was invited to evoke a city, a region, a place to which he was attached. One hundred and ten authors—including Roland Barthes, Roger Caillois, Milan Kundera, Louis Guilloux, Gabriel García Márquez, Françoise Sagan, Georges Simenon, and Michel Tournier—responded positively to the suggestion.

Two months earlier, Charles Silvestre had seen Jean Genet, who had come to submit his latest article to the editorial office, and had the idea of suggesting he write the first text of the series. To ask Genet, whose origins he was unaware of, what "country" meant to him, was daring; but the writer, amused by the theme, accepted the proposition. He promised an article for the appointed day and disappeared. He didn't appear again at the paper till the day before publication, when the editor had given up hope of seeing him again: "I wrote it, but I'm not sure of the result," he said to Charles Silvestre. "He asked," Silvestre said later, "only one thing: to reread the typeset text. That night, he returned, took the proof, went over it line by line and made just one correction. The typographer had spontaneously set a capital S in Stoléru's name. In fact, Genet had come back just for that. To make sure the lower-case letter of the minister was kept." ("Pour un petit 's'" [For a small "s"], *L'Humanité*, April 16, 1986, p. 16.)

Even more than to Chartres cathedral, long admired by the author (the title *Notre-Dame-des-Fleurs* [Our lady of the flowers] led us to think of the book as a small Romanesque cathedral), Genet's article is devoted to a reflection on the idea of "country" [*pays*] and "fatherland" [*patrie*]. If only because of what is at stake in these terms in Genet's work, this text can be considered as crucial and deserves a reading that is all the more attentive, since its seeming simplicity dissimulates a complex thought in which irony is always present.

Genet will say some time later to B. Poirot-Delpech that he had written this text "a little bit as a joke." See Jean Genet, *L'ennemi déclaré: Textes et entretiens*, edited by Albert Dichy, *Ouevres complètes*, vol. 6 (Paris: Gallimard, 1991), p. 234. This dimension was not always recognized. Thus, Jacques Henrie could write, taking the homage to a region literally: "Here's this old convict, the outcast, the *maudit* writer ostracized from the 'national community,' who suddenly becomes the bard of the Fatherland, inclines toward Pétainist ideology like any Marchais or Chirac. . . . Barrès or Péguy couldn't have done better." (See "Monsieur Jean Genet, nouveau patriote" [Mr. Jean Genet, new patriot], *Libération*, September 21, 1977, p. 14.)

More crafty than it seems, Genet's text actually takes the opposite of the subject that is imposed on him and works to undo the idea of fatherland. Riddled with a multitude of underlying questions (immigrant workers, foreigners, Palestinians, Sahraouis, the Third World, etc.) and with references to the latest current events (the campaign for the revalorization of manual labor, for which posters covered the capital's walls in 1977), connected to each other and to the central theme, it offers much more than a historical reminiscence: a reading of History at full gallop—reread from a political angle.

That is, moreover, what the original heading of the article reveals, the first draft of which bears the following title: "Micro-treatise on mini-politics." We'll give here a few fragments, not previously reprinted, of this initial version (one copy of which is preserved in the Genet collection), in which the definition of "fatherland" according to Genet finds its first formulation:

"The true fatherland, any fatherland, is a wound. Yesterday, the French fatherland was both scattered and united during the Occupation. The Palestinian fatherland exists today because it is wounded.

"If every fatherland had to be made up of men and women who knew each other, almost by name, it could be made up of only a limited number—one that each person could count and know. Extensive calculations give us the number three thousand four hundred twenty-seven men and women. Maybe less, never more.

"To know oneself. What is our yardstick?

"One can postulate a fatherland if it is composed of: eight Moroccans, seven Japanese, eleven Germans, fifteen Cubans, a few Frenchmen, one guy from Beauce ..."

Published on page 2 of the daily paper, Genet's article was illustrated with three photographs of Chartres cathedral and introduced by a general presentation of the author by Jean-Pierre Léonardini, listing his main works and defenses of the Palestinians and of American Blacks that he'd recently published in the paper's columns. Here we have preserved the fragmentary layout of the manuscript, in which each paragraph is clearly separated from the others by a line.

SOURCES: Entretien avec Charles Silvestre [Interview with Charles Silvestre], Archives Charles Silvestre, Alexandre Bouglione, Jean Genet Collection / I.M.E.C.

## *"The Brothers Karamazov"*

Text written at an undetermined date (between 1975 and 1980), submitted to Gallimard in 1981, and published in *La nouvelle revue française* in October 1986. The text presented here follows the manuscript.

### BACKGROUND NOTES

The date of the writing of this text is still difficult to fix precisely. It was written following a reading of Dostoyevsky's novel during a stay in Apulia, around 1975. This reading is recalled by the author in his interview with Hubert Fichte (see p. 119): "I can tell you that I spent two months reading *The Brothers Karamazov*. I was in bed. I was in Italy, I'd read one page and then . . . I'd have to think for two hours, then start again, it's enormous and exhausting."

It's not until 1981 that Genet confided these manuscript pages to Laurent Boyer at Gallimard, "for Georges Lambrichs to publish in *La N.R.F.* [La nouvelle revue française]." Then, seeing the typeset text, he changed his mind, saying it was all a joke. . . . But many years later, when he was writing *Un captif amoureux* [Prisoner of love], he returned to the copy of his article, which he planned to publish at the same time. He didn't make any corrections to it.

This text, published in the months following his death and the appearance of the book, is thus indeed a finished text that was written alongside his public statements and that occupies a separate place in this collection. We chose to include it because it demonstrates what *Un captif amoureux* amply shows: the development of a contrapuntal poetics in Genet's work and, more profoundly, as an accompaniment, of a reflection on politics.

No doubt the text must first be considered as a homage to Dostoyevsky. Cited, with hardly any explanation, in several interviews, the Russian novelist seems a major literary reference for Genet—just as Giacometti is for sculpture, Rembrandt for painting and Mozart, perhaps, for music.

But if this text offers a precise and original reading of *The Bro-*

*thers Karamazov,* it also opens up a larger perspective: it outlines an actual theory of the novel and—if one refers to the final references to music, painting, and theater—of the work of art in general. In this sense, one can read between the lines, in these few pages held in reserve by the author, a sort of "poetic art" from which his final works stem.

The spacing of the paragraphs is reprinted here in accordance with the manuscript. Since the manuscript bears no title, we have used the one from the typeset edition the author had in his possession. With the slightly different title "Une Lecture des Frères Karamazov" [A reading of the Brothers Karamazov] this text was published for the first time in the October 1986 edition of *La nouvelle revue française* (no. 405, pp. 69–72).

SOURCES: Interview with Laurent Boyer, Archives Gallimard, Alexandre Bouglione.

# Sources

The texts gathered in *Fragments of the Artwork* originally appeared in French in the following places and under the following copyrights:

From *Fragments . . . et autres textes* [Fragments . . . and other texts], © Editions Gallimard 1990; English-language rights reserved by the author's estate.

1. 'adame Miroir [1948]
2. Letter to Leonor Fini [1950]
3. Jean Cocteau [1950]
4. Fragments ... [1954]
5. Letter to Jean-Jacques Pauvert [1954]

From *Oeuvres complètes* [Complete works], vol. 5, © Editions Gallimard 1979. English-language rights reserved by the author's estate.

6. The Studio of Alberto Giacometti [1957, first published in 1958 by Marc Barbezat, L'Arbalète]
7. The Tightrope Walker [1958, first published in 1958 by Marc Barbezat, L'Arbalète]
8. Rembrandt's Secret [1958]

From *Oeuvres complètes*, vol. 4, © Editions Gallimard 1968. English-language rights reserved by the author's estate.

9. What Remains of a Rembrandt Torn into Little Squares All the Same Size and Shot Down the Toilet [1967]

10. That Strange Word ... [1967]

11. Interview with Hubert Fichte [1975]

12. Chartres Cathedral, A "Bird's-Eye" View [1977]

13. *"The Brothers Karamazov"* [1981]

# Notes

## 1. 'adame Miroir

1. Episode of the Rose. The Image has no rose in his belt. With his teeth, the dancer playing the role of the Image tears away this rose, runs off, and keeps it in his mouth.

## 4. Fragments ...

1. "Strange loves! A twilight smell isolates you. But it is less the disheveled monster of your interlaced bodies than its image multiplied in the mirrors of a bordello—or your delicate brain?—that troubles you! Dripping with sweat, you climb back up from those absurdly distant lands: you had capsized in yourself where flight is surest, your drunkenness swelling to the point of exploding—from your sole and reciprocal exhalation. Loves, name these games of reflections that are exhausted, shouted out endlessly on the walls of gilded rooms."

Thus speaks an oblique reason that, fascinated, watches death appear in each accident. Name, exhaust these games and come back to the air. You recognize and accept the smell of the pieces of shit that, hemming it, remain beneath the index fingernail. It is slight and sad, dawn of sterile loves. Not nauseous, but indicative of exception. "Amuse yourself when others are bored stiff" is the expression of a regret. Your memory preserves it, so you float in a halo of subtle shame and reprobation: the most despised of the places of the body is not ennobled, but cherished. Such clear, such pure faces, if my cruelty doesn't make tears come to them—and snot: it's this sweet, sad smell I want them to be enveloped in when they go away.

"If I tear out a piece, yes, like an aniseed . . ." but if I cram your shit, handsome monsters, it is not into you that I plunge it, it is from you that I escape for your image, infinitely multiplied, where I wander.

2. By the eagle, transport of a lamb: in the air, his four feet suddenly useless. The audacity of theft is in the fixed, round eye! The most consoling image, and for us, this evening, the most effective will be the idea of Ganymede lifted by the bird. Stretched out on the unmade bed, the adolescent finally abandons himself and lets the slow, majestic wingspan develop. Brought to earth, bitten on the neck, calmed gently but profoundly by the god, he is ravished. Lightning! Thunderbolts! No. The eagle is embroidered on a shroud where the child expires. "Come, you will be the cupbearer of the gods." Tousled, scarcely intimidated, you enter heaven to serve the Queers.

3. Even though my entire activity as a thief was only the visible stylization, led into the world of action, of an erotic theme, so much so that I went about it in a poetic aura, that is, gratuitous and useless, my lovers, unable to be anything but apparent supports, were capricious ornaments without practical value, with no other virtue than that of uselessness and luxury: my thieves, my sailors, my soldiers, my criminals? no: their image.

4. I will call "real" any event that can be the starting point for a morality, that is to say, for a rule on which the relationships of all men rest. The word that seems able to express them might be the word "equity." An unreal attitude is one that logically leads to aesthetics.

5. I no longer ignore the fact that from one single fact that cannot be led to a system of morality, you must extract, if you are coherent, an aesthetics.

6. With my cold chisel, words, detached from language, neat blocks, are also tombs. They hold prisoner the confused nostalgia of an action that men accomplished and that words, bloody at the time, mean to name. Here they are silent. The deed was accomplished elsewhere, in mythical times. Words preserve only a faint light from those times. Nothing more imprecise than the word "ceremony," except for whatever it still retains of rigor, order and earthly power. Words also get their qualities from those powers that consecrate them and to which they refer, but which would give so many more powers to the powerful if words referred to an order that was consecrated by song.

7. The words used for my construction lose their power of commu-

nication. They are finite, hemmed in as much as possible by their own contours, and I will make sure that they refer poorly to the objects they name, that of these objects there will remain captive only the most ghostly appearance, but that the word is colored with my anguish, and that, from the relationship of each of them, tomb without contents, there rises up an abstract construct possessing force and meaning.

8. Isn't the least wretched thing the pederast can do, if he picks a boyfriend, to impose on him a fate he can't take on in his own body? No doubt this is still a "reflective" way to live, to choose a reflection for oneself—or an earthly representation—or a delegate—that one projects onto the world when one thinks it is himself, but, aided by some nobility of the soul, as the boyfriend awakens, suffers, lives on the earth, the pederast must strictly try to annihilate himself till he is nothing but a beam of light guiding his delegate, a breath inspiring him, the soul of a body and of a soul, to the point of being only an "idea of infinite misery." Knowing how vain are the prestigious rags of the world, what I have just called "nobility" still seems base when you use it to cover the shoulders—even if they are muscular—of an adolescent. It is to offer him an empty power. If not to kill him, what can I demand from a friend whose love I need—and with him, the world's recognition?

9. Sign of pederast passion: it is the possession of an object that will have no other fate than the fate required by the lover. The loved one becomes an object charged, in this world, with representing death (the lover). (Sign of the obsession of the Emperor Heliogabalus whose coachman wears the attributes—robe, cloak, necklace—of power—when the Emperor lives alone, obscure, secret, in an empty room in the palace.) The lover charges a servant with living in his place. Not living, appearing. Neither one nor the other lives. The loved one does not adorn the lover, he "reproduces" him. The loved one is then sterilized if he lives unhealthily according to this obsession that haunts the lover.

10. There are enough lost children, I tell myself, I will steal one of them. Let him live in my place. Let him take charge of my fate. What fate, if I want to be dead? Let him take charge of my death. Absurd scenario: sealed in a vault, pensive, determined, desperate—with my love, I direct my weak ambassador among the living. He will live my hatred. Paradoxically, my rupture is perpetuated. Will he have to love me? First he must bear evil: a criminal child will travel through the world. Viciously turned on him, it is from me he awaits a spark. If he kills, he is silent: prison, scaffold, hard labor, so many deaths he will live in my

place. But to accept our mortal injunction this way, one must oneself be dead. The lost child was dead already. His secret carnival was not ours, we couldn't recognize it, nor he ours. Alas, it is only through love that he could obey our orders. And we, will we call "love" this rigor that comes from the prison cell that forced us to lead him to death, to invent evils for him, a moral code, the habits of death among men?

## 7. The Tightrope Walker

1. The most moving are the ones that withdraw into a sign of grotesque derision: a hairstyle, a certain kind of moustache, rings, shoes. . . . For an instant, their entire life rushes there, and detail sparkles: suddenly, it goes out: that is because all the glory that was brought there has just withdrawn into that secret region, finally bringing solitude.

## 10. That Strange Word ...

1. This page no longer exists.

## 11. Interview with Hubert Fichte

All notes to this interview are by Albert Dichy except for translator's additions, which are inserted in brackets.

1. A first meeting between Hubert Fichte and Genet had taken place the day before, on December 18, at Éditions Gallimard. Although their conversation was not recorded, Genet refers back to it several times throughout the interview.

2. Various unions and parties of the Left organized a coordinated demonstration on December 18 to protest "the antisocial and repressive politics of power." The same day, there was also a march by the "Comité national pour la libération des soldats et militaires emprisonnés" [National committee for the liberation of imprisoned soldiers and servicemen], supported by all the organizations of the far Left.

3. See "Entretien avec Michèle Monceaux," *L'ennemi déclaré*, p. 346.

4. The principal architect of Versailles was in fact the nephew of François Mansart, Hardouin-Mansart (1646–1708), who took over the construction in 1678 and finished it in 1695.

5. Oscar Niemeyer, born in Rio de Janeiro in 1907, a disciple of Le Corbusier, was, with Lucio Costa, the main architect of Brasilia, built

between 1957 and 1960. Already during its first year, the new city was surrounded by a vast shantytown, the "Bandeirante"; inhabited by the families of workers engaged in the construction of the city, it grew as the city itself grew.

6. The Dominican chapel at Vence (called the Chapel of the Rosary) was completed in 1951. It is considered one of Matisse's most successful works and was constructed entirely under his supervision, from the architectural design to the making of the furniture and the conception of the liturgical vestments.

7. Genet is referring to his visit to Japan in November 1969.

8. A painting by Goya (1792).

9. It was shortly after this reading that Genet wrote the text *"The Brothers Karamazov"* (see p. 159).

10. On July 31, 1962, the Hamburg court rejected a demand presented by the public prosecutor's office to seize and ban the German translation of *Our Lady of the Flowers* for "obscenity and outrage to public morals." This decision led to a revision of the censorship laws and is a landmark in the history of erotic and homosexual literature in Germany. (See Helmut Boysen, "Genet acquitté," *L'Express*, no. 586, September 6, 1962, p. 21.)

11. More precisely, in the village of Alligny, in the Morvan region, the northeastern border of France shared with Belgium, Luxembourg, and Germany.

12. He had been summoned by the Immigration and Naturalization Services to justify his entry into the United States without a visa.

13. See "May Day Speech," *L'ennemi déclaré*, p. 344, n. 2.

14. "The Head of Hair," poem 23 of *The Flowers of Evil.*

15. Genet is referring to the two *Discours concernant le jugement de Louis XVI* [Discourses concerning the judgment of Louis XVI], delivered to the National Convention, the first on November 13, 1790, the second on December 27, 1793.

16. This is a general interpretation of the second discourse of Saint-Just, not a citation.

17. Louis Aragon, "Avez-vous giflé un mort?" [Did you slap a dead man?], in *Un cadavre* [A corpse], a tract of 1924, p. 4.

18. Sartre traveled to the Soviet Union in 1954.

19. "Fatherland or death."

20. This is the first line of the sonnet "The Tomb of Edgar Poe."

21. Genet went to the Odéon with Roger Blin on May 15, 1968, the

day of the "taking" of the theater. See also "Entretien avec Nigel Williams," *L'ennemi déclaré*, p. 297.

22. [In "Et pourquoi pas la sottise en bretelles?" (A Fool in suspenders: Why not?), *L'ennemi déclaré*, p. 369, n. 6, the editor writes that, just after being elected president, "On May 27, 1974, Giscard d'Estaing led a procession, on foot, up the Champs-Élysées, (toward the Place de l'Étoile and the Arc de Triomphe), to celebrate the formation of the new government." In the essay, Genet points out that this is exactly contrary to de Gaulle's triumphant procession in 1945 *down* the avenue, in the opposite direction—*Trans.*]

23. After examining the FBI archives, Edmund White was able to state without any doubt that Genet's presence among the Black Panthers had been noted from the day of his arrival in the United States.

24. George Wallace, a right-wing politician, ran several times for president of the United States.

25. Salvador Allende, elected president of Chile in 1970, installed a socialist government before being killed in September 1973 during the military takeover led by General Pinochet.

26. ITT: International Telephone and Telegraph, an American company set up in Chile and implicated in the putsch.

27. In September 1971, Buffet and Bontemps, who were being held at the Clairveaux prison, took a police sergeant and a nurse hostage, then killed them later. Despite a campaign against the death penalty led by a number of intellectuals, they were executed on November 28, 1972.

28. See *The Thief's Journal* for a similar story.

29. On this question, see the reflection developed throughout "Le rouge et le noir" [The red and the black], *L'ennemi déclaré*, pp. 101-4.

30. This is probably a veiled reference to the suicide of Abdallah, for which Genet may have felt at least partially responsible. [Abdallah Bentaga, a young Algerian acrobat, was Genet's companion for a number of years in the late '50s and early '60s. Genet personally trained him to be a high-wire artist and wrote for him the short text entitled "The Tightrope Walker." Apparently distraught at being replaced in Genet's affections by another young companion, Abdallah committed suicide in March 1964—*Trans.*]

31. The Panathenaea was an important Athenian festival in honor of Athena.

32. *Funeral Rites* and *Querelle* were also written after Genet left prison for the last time.

33. Genet's *Oeuvres complètes*, in fact, began to appear in 1951.

34. In the margin of the transcript, Fichte wrote the word sait [know] above suis [am], which renders the sentence more coherent. [I have incorporated this change into the text. The original typed version gives: "We'd have to talk about what I am not"—*Trans.*]

35. Potlatch (an ethnological term referring to practices of Indians of the Pacific Northwest): a ceremony involving the ostentatious destruction of goods.

36. A reference to the main character of Genet's novel *Querelle*.

37. Pasolini had recently been murdered, on November 1, 1976, in a suburb of Rome by a seventeen-year-old apprentice baker.

38. See a first version of this story in "Entretien avec Madaleine Gobeil," *L'ennemi déclaré*, p. 19 and p. 334, n. 14.

39. It is highly unlikely that up to 1939 Genet had read nothing but pulp novels: one need only consult his letters from 1937 to Anne Bloch, his "German friend" in Czechoslovakia (published in Hamburg by Merlin Verlag under the title *Chère Madame* [Dear madam]. Behind this coy gesture of the autodidact there is no doubt something deeper: a refusal to be allied with the official culture.

40. Genet was placed in the Mettray Penal Colony from September 1926 to March 1929.

41. A sedative that Genet took almost every day beginning in the mid-1950s.

42. Bernard Huguenin, financial director of Éditions Gallimard.

43. Genet had a long stopover in Karachi in early 1968 while on his first trip to Japan.

44. Mohammed El Katrani, whom Genet met in September 1974 in Tangier, remained close to Genet until his death. (A note in the unpublished film script, *La nuit venue* [Nightfall], written in 1976 and 1977, mentions that the script was based "on an original idea of M. El Katrani.")

45. Rosa Luxemburg, Marxist thinker and revolutionary, who was arrested and executed during "Red Week" in Berlin on January 15, 1919.

46. Lindbergh had landed in Paris on May 21, 1927.

47. In order to leave the Mettray colony, Genet enlisted in the army and volunteered to serve with the troops in the eastern Mediterranean. Placed with a company of sappers and miners, he was stationed in Damascus from February to December 1930; at the time, he was nineteen years old.

48. This is the one time that Genet, thanks to a curious slip (not corrected when he reread the text), pronounces the name of General Goudot, for whom he had worked as a secretary for three months in Morocco, in the summer of 1931.

General Gouraud, frequently mentioned by Genet, though he never served under him, was High Commissioner in Syria from 1919 to 1923 and remained a legendary figure in the region for a long time after. But it was under the command of General Gamelin that Damascus was bombed at the end of 1925 during the insurrection of the Jebel Druses, four years or so before Genet went there. (See Albert Dichy and Pascal Fouché, *Jean Genet, essai de chronologie* [Bibliothèque de Littérature Française, 1988], pp. 131–41.)

49. After taking power, Castro took very repressive measures against homosexuality.

50. In July 1970, Huey Newton, cofounder of the Black Panther Party, published an important article in *The Black Panther* on questions concerning homosexuality and feminism as these relate to revolution. This article may have been inspired by the letter from Genet to Bobby Seale mentioned here.

51. Cocteau testified on Genet's behalf, on July 19, 1943, at a trial in which Genet was in danger of receiving a life sentence, and this testimony was decisive. In it, Cocteau claimed that Genet was "the greatest writer of the age." (See *Jean Genet, essai de chronologie*, pp. 211–17.)

52. Genet was working on sketches of what would become *Prisoner of Love*. At the time, the title of the work—a title that had obsessed Genet since the 1950s, but that he ended up never using—was "Death." (On the form this work was to take, see Massin, Continuo, B.L.F.C./I.M.E.C., 1988, pp. 27–28).

## *12. Chartres Cathedral*

All notes to this essay are by Albert Dichy.

1. Nara, ancient imperial city of Japan where Buddhism began to develop in the sixth and seventh centuries. Considered the cradle of Japanese civilization, the city has many Buddhist temples and shrines.

2. The "right to difference": slogan used during a 1977 government campaign aiming to reassert the value of manual labor.

3. *The Tree of Jesse*: twelfth-century stained-glass window on the western façade of the cathedral, representing Christ's genealogical tree

going back to Jesse, father of David.

4. The government campaign to which note 2 refers was conducted mainly through posters.

5. Lionel Stoléru was, in 1977, the secretary of state in the cabinet of Raymond Barre. He was in charge of a campaign to revalorize manual labor. (On the reasons for the small letter beginning his name, see the above annotations.)

6. It was due to the initiative of André Malraux, minister of culture for General de Gaulle, that the first great international exhibitions took place.

7. Saying attributed to Benjamin Franklin.

8. A large exhibition devoted to ancient Egypt was being held for a season at the Louvre.

9. It's the word *rebus* [not *rebut*] that is in the published text and in the author's manuscript. We preferred to give the word that seemed required by the meaning of the sentence—although a "rebus" has just enough meaning to cause some trouble.

10. Sahraoui: supporter of independence for the Western Sahara, territory shared by Morocco and Mauritania, and presently integrated into Morocco. Supported by Algeria, the Polisario Liberation Front proclaimed, on February 28, 1976, the Sahraoui Republic and organized an armed opposition.

11. Dacca (official spelling since 1983: Dhaka), capital of Bangladesh, one of the poorest countries in the world.

12. *Douar* (Arab word from the Maghreb): encampment of tents arranged in circles.

13. In March 1975, the Cuban army (supported by the Soviet Union) intervened in the violent civil war that was starting in Angola.

## *13. "The Brothers Karamazov"*

1. The typeset edition of the text gives here "*L'humour*" [The humor]. We are using the version of the manuscript that leaves out the definite article—*Ed.*

2. See "Rembrandt's Secret," p, 89: "the sleeve in *The Jewish Bride* is an abstract painting." This 1666 painting is also entitled *Isaac and Rebecca*—*Ed.*

M E R I D I A N

*Crossing Aesthetics*

Jean Genet, *Fragments of the Artwork*

Shoshana Felman, *The Scandal of the Speaking Body: Don Juan with J. L. Austin, or Seduction in Two Languages*

Peter Szondi, *Celan Studies*

Neil Hertz, *George Eliot's Pulse*

Maurice Blanchot, *The Book to Come*

Susannah Young-ah Gottlieb, *Regions of Sorrow: Anxiety and Messianism in Hannah Arendt and W. H. Auden*

Jacques Derrida, *Without Alibi*, edited by Peggy Kamuf

Cornelius Castoriadis, *On Plato's 'Statesman'*

Jacques Derrida, *Who's Afraid of Philosophy? Right to Philosophy 1*

Peter Szondi, *An Essay on the Tragic*

Peter Fenves, *Arresting Language: From Leibniz to Benjamin*

Jill Robbins, ed., *Is It Righteous to Be? Interviews with Emmanuel Levinas*

Louis Marin, *Of Representation*

Daniel Payot, *The Architect and the Philosopher*

J. Hillis Miller, *Speech Acts in Literature*

Maurice Blanchot, *Faux pas*

Jean-Luc Nancy, *Being Singular Plural*

Maurice Blanchot / Jacques Derrida, *The Instant of My Death / Demeure: Fiction and Testimony*

Niklas Luhmann, *Art as a Social System*

Emmanual Levinas, *God, Death, and Time*

Ernst Bloch, *The Spirit of Utopia*

Giorgio Agamben, *Potentialities: Collected Essays in Philosophy*

Ellen S. Burt, *Poetry's Appeal: French Nineteenth-Century Lyric and the Political Space*

Jacques Derrida, *Adieu to Emmanuel Levinas*

Werner Hamacher, *Premises: Essays on Philosophy and Literature from Kant to Celan*

Aris Fioretos, *The Gray Book*

Deborah Esch, *In the Event: Reading Journalism, Reading Theory*

Winfried Menninghaus, *In Praise of Nonsense: Kant and Bluebeard*

Giorgio Agamben, *The Man Without Content*

Giorgio Agamben, *The End of the Poem: Essays in Poetics*

Theodor W. Adorno, *Sound Figures*

Louis Marin, *Sublime Poussin*

Philippe Lacoue-Labarthe, *Poetry as Experience*

Ernst Bloch, *Literary Essays*

Jacques Derrida, *Resistances of Psychoanalysis*

Marc Froment-Meurice, *That Is to Say: Heidegger's Poetics*

Francis Ponge, *Soap*

Philippe Lacoue-Labarthe, *Typography: Mimesis, Philosophy, Politics*

Giorgio Agamben, *Homo Sacer: Sovereign Power and Bare Life*

Emmanuel Levinas, *Of God Who Comes to Mind*

Bernard Stiegler, Technics and Time, *1: The Fault of Epimetheus*

Werner Hamacher, *pleroma—Reading in Hegel*

Serge Leclaire, *Psychoanalyzing: On the Order of the Unconscious and the Practice of the Letter*

Serge Leclaire, *A Child Is Being Killed: On Primary Narcissism and the Death Drive*

Sigmund Freud, *Writings on Art and Literature*

Cornelius Castoriadis, *World in Fragments: Writings on Politics, Society, Psychoanalysis, and the Imagination*

Thomas Keenan, *Fables of Responsibility: Aberrations and Predicaments in Ethics and Politics*

Emmanuel Levinas, *Proper Names*

Alexander García Düttmann, *At Odds with AIDS: Thinking and Talking About a Virus*

Maurice Blanchot, *Friendship*

Jean-Luc Nancy, *The Muses*

Massimo Cacciari, *Posthumous People: Vienna at the Turning Point*

David E. Wellbery, *The Specular Moment: Goethe's Early Lyric and the Beginnings of Romanticism*

Edmond Jabès, *The Little Book of Unsuspected Subversion*

Hans-Jost Frey, *Studies in Poetic Discourse: Mallarmé, Baudelaire, Rimbaud, Hölderlin*

Pierre Bourdieu, *The Rules of Art: Genesis and Structure of the Literary Field*

Nicolas Abraham, *Rhythms: On the Work, Translation, and Psychoanalysis*

Jacques Derrida, *On the Name*

David Wills, *Prosthesis*

Maurice Blanchot, *The Work of Fire*

Jacques Derrida, *Points . . . : Interviews, 1974–1994*

J. Hillis Miller, *Topographies*

Philippe Lacoue-Labarthe, *Musica Ficta (Figures of Wagner)*

Jacques Derrida, *Aporias*

Emmanuel Levinas, *Outside the Subject*

Jean-François Lyotard, *Lessons on the Analytic of the Sublime*

Peter Fenves, *"Chatter": Language and History in Kierkegaard*

Jean-Luc Nancy, *The Experience of Freedom*

Jean-Joseph Goux, *Oedipus, Philosopher*

Haun Saussy, *The Problem of a Chinese Aesthetic*

Jean-Luc Nancy, *The Birth to Presence*